Gra
Tast
Christmas

DIANNE C. EVANS

ISBN #0-9615089-0-6
1st Printing:, 2006
Printed in Korea
Granny illustrations by Cheryl Benner
Delafield Stamps are used with the written permission of
Delafield Stamp Company, Delafield, WI

CONTENTS

Over the river and through the wood,
To grandmother's house we go;
The horse knows the way
To carry the sleigh,
Through the white and drifted snow.

Over the river and through the wood,
Oh how the wind does blow;
It stings the toes
And bites the nose,
As over the ground we go.

Lydia Maria Child (1802-1880)

Introduction:

ack in 1976, I wrote a little Christmas cookbook called "A Taste of Christmas". I took it to the Power's Crossroads Arts & Crafts show in Newnan Georgia and much to my surprise, my first printing of 1000 copies almost *sold out* in the 3-day Labor Day week-end event!

The following week, a sales rep, who had seen my little 64 page paperback stapled cookbook, came to see me and wanted me to re-print the book, presenting me with a more professional, polished looking cover. I took his advice, *and* his new cover, and reprinted 5000 more copies. He then introduced me to Dot Gibson in Waycross, GA, who was just getting started in her cookbook distributing business. To this day, Dot and her son Gil are still one of my best distributors.

In June 1977, I participated in "Stay & See Georgia", a week-long Chamber of Commerce/Travel Industry event held at Lenox Square Mall in Atlanta. I took 500 gift-size loaves of homemade breads and of course, my newly reprinted "A Taste of Christmas" cookbook. A couple of weeks after the show, a representative and his camera man from a Georgia magazine, "Brown's Guide to Georgia" showed up at my front door in Thomasville, GA and wanted to do a story for their magazine. (I think the 500 loaves of bread got their editor's attention!)

Well, while we talked, his photographer took pictures of me baking loaves of bread, and sure enough, my story appeared in the next addition of Brown's Guide to Georgia--quite a thrill.

After that, I was encouraged to do a second edition of the "Taste", but never got around to it. I went into the catering business, and later ran the Horseshoe Plantation Main House in Tallahassee, FL, the results of which produced a plantation-type cookbook, titled "Bobwhite Quail & Buttermilk Biscuits".

To regress a little, I started out in the catering business very much like Paula Deen. In fact, I was living in Thomasville, Georgia, a neighboring town of Paula's Albany, when I started catering in 1972. I had just had two babies, 15 months apart and wanted to stay home with them, rather than continue working at the radio station for my husband. With four other children in school, I still needed to make the extra money. So I decided to do what I had read you should do when you want to go into business, "do what you do best". With my large family and having a mother who had taught me the love of baking, that was no contest!

I went to Tallahassee and took a Wilton decorating class. I then called all of the ladies in Thomasville that I knew were selling cakes out of their home, anonymously of course, and asked them if they used cake mixes, real butter and what they charged. Armed with this information, I decided to use my sour cream pound cake recipe for all of all my decorated cakes, use "real" butter and buy fresh eggs from my friend, Hattie, across the road, who raised chickens! Not only was I going to bake the best cakes but I was going to charge more than the other bakers. I named my little business "Patchwork Pantry" and took out a nice ad in the local newspaper. Soon I was baking 8 birthday cakes every Saturday, catering weddings and all kinds of parties. I also catered business lunches in the Corporate Business Park and had a thriving business when the Horseshoe Plantation job came along.

Horseshoe Plantation had just been leased, and later bought, by Oilman, Fred Hamilton, of Denver, CO and Campbell Soup CEO, John Dorrance, Jr. of Gladwyne, PA. Their hunting guests included H. J. Heinz, Jr., Georgia Gov. George Busbee, Colorado Gov. John Love, Texas Oilman, T. Boone Pickens, Gen. William Westmoreland and many other notables.

Just from that little "Patchwork Pantry" beginning, a whole new world opened up for us, cooking from New York to Palm Beach, for the rich and sometimes famous.

I've come full circle now, back to my first love, writing cookbooks. My new books focus on a "Granny" theme and are spiced up with a little Granny "tongue in check" humor throughout.

As with the first, in our "Granny's" series, "Turnip Greens, Ham Hocks & Granny's Buns", these Southern Christmas favorites are simple, easy-to-follow and geared toward the beginner as well as bringing back warm and fuzzy memories for the seasoned cook.

In this edition, you'll find an expanded version of our handy Kitchen Arithmetic section and again, it's in the front of the book so it will be at your fingertips. You'll find more of Granny's cooking tips too, along with some of our favorite family Christmas photos and a new feature, old-fashioned Christmas Carols with the music.

One of the great joys of Christmas is delving into some wonderful food with those you love. I sincerely hope this book will assist you in making that happen.

Dianne Evans

The Duke & Duchess of Windsor, shown here on the Horseshoe Plantation lawn, were relatives of the original owners, The George Bakers', of New York.
They visited Horseshoe many times during the 1950's and were often seen shopping in downtown Thomasville, GA.

Yuletide Menus

#1
Treating the Caroliers

Meg's Decorated Sugar Cookies, 105
Mini Cherry Cheesecakes, 106
Reindeer Munchies, 61
Hot Buttered Rum (for the adults), 37
Holiday Hot Chocolate (for the children), 43

#2
Ice Skating Party Treats

Spinach/Artichoke Dip, 31
(purchased toasted baguette bread slices)
Jezebel Sauce over Cream Cheese, 33
Coconut Pound Cake with Coconut Glaze, 146
Hello Dolly Bars, 95
Mulled Cider, 38

#3
Holiday House Get-together

Smoked Turkey & Slivers of Baked Ham (purchased)
Mini Croissants (purchased)
Condiments (mustard, mayo, etc.)
Smoky Cheeseball, with assorted crackers, 21
Spinach-Crabmeat Dip, with veggie tray, 29
Pecan Tassies, 161   Mini Cheesecakes, 106
Toasted Pecans, 34
Christmas Wassail, 38

#4
Friends Holiday Get-together
Seafood Casserole, 197
Seasoned Green Beans, 195
Tossed Salad of Mixed Greens & Vegetables
Tray of Lemon Tassies, 160

Variety Gift Boxes
Buy large muffin cup liners in paper or foil at a craft
store's cake department. Make your treats small, fill
your paper cups and arrange in a nice flat gift box. Use
the pretty gold doilies to line recycled plastic contains.
They usually have a clear lid. You can even buy large
round foil divided plates with clear plastic dome covers.
Many good gift packaging items can be found at
Michael's Craft Stores.

Suggested Combinations:
Be sure and make the cookies and candies bite-size
and cut the bars into 1-inch squares.

#1
Tiny Gingerbread Cut-out Cookies, 94
Park's Bakery Brownies, 100
Mother's Sugared Pecans, 61
Coconut Balls, 67

#2
Toasted Pecans, 34
Tracey's Rocky Road Fudge, 70
Strawberry Divinity Squares, 66
White Peanut Butter Fudge, 51
Santa's Whiskers, 84

Chocolate Peanut Butter Balls, 60
Aunt Judy's Heavenly Bits, 83
Fruitcake Cookies, 98
Pecan Log Slices, 59
Jammies, 82

12 Delicious Treats to Take to Shut-Ins:

1. Instant Russian Tea Mix, 42
2. Holiday Hot Chocolate Mix, 43
3. Sleighride Mocha Coffee Mix, 42

Put mix, about 1 cup, in a plastic bag, secure with a bread wrapper "twistie", include a cinnamon stick for stirring and place in a pretty Holiday mug. Wrap the mug in cellophane and don't forget the directions for use. A little bag of homemade holiday cookies would be nice.

4. Snickerdoodles, 91
5. Banana Nut Bread, 247
6. Date Nut Gift Bread, 224
7. Aunt Judy's Heavenly Bits, 83
8. Chocolate Syrup Brownies, 99
9. A small jar of your homemade pepper jelly, 32
together with an 8 oz. pkg. of cream cheese and a small box of crackers; all in a basket lined with Christmas fabric.
10. Zucchini Gift Bread, 237
11. A basket of homemade Blueberry Muffins, 228
12. One dozen Hello Dolly Bars, 95

Kitchen Arithmetic

Handy Substitutions

1 cup self-rising flour = 1 cup all-purpose flour plus
1 tsp. baking powder & ½ tsp. salt

1 cup cake flour = 1 cup *minus* 2 Tbsp. all-purpose flour

1 cup all-purpose flour = 1 cup *plus* 2 Tbsp. cake flour

1 teaspoon baking powder = ½ tsp. cream of tartar plus
¼ tsp. baking soda

1 tablespoon tapioca (for thickening) = 1½ Tbsp. all-purpose flour

1 tablespoon cornstarch (for thickening) = 2 Tbsp. flour

Sugar, Granulated, 1 cup = 1 cup packed brown sugar *or*
2 cups sifted powdered sugar

> **Powdered, 1 cup** = 1 cup granulated sugar plus
> 1 tsp. cornstarch. Pulse in food processor until
> powder.

> **Brown sugar, 1 cup packed** = 1 cup granulated
> sugar plus 1½ Tbsp. molasses

Corn Syrup, 1½ cups = 1 cup sugar plus ½ cup water

Honey, 1 cup = 1¼ cups sugar plus ¼ cup water

Corn syrup, honey and molasses are interchangeable

Allspice Mix, 1 teaspoon = ½ tsp. cinnamon plus ⅛ tsp.
ground cloves

Apple Pie Spice Mix, 1 teaspoon = ½ tsp. cinnamon,
¼ tsp. nutmeg, ⅛ tsp. allspice & a dash of ginger

Gingerbread Spice Mix = 3 tsp. ground ginger, 1 tsp.
cinnamon & 1 tsp. ground cloves. Mix all together
and keep in an airtight jar and measure out
amount as needed

Ginger: Fresh, grated, 1 Tbsp = ⅛ tsp. ground
Crystallized, 1 Tbsp. = ⅛ tsp. ground

Pumpkin Pie Spice Mix, 1 teaspoon = ½ tsp. cinnamon,
¼ tsp. ginger, ⅛ tsp. allspice, & ⅛ tsp. nutmeg

Chocolate:

> **Semi-sweet, 1 ounce square** = 1 ounce unsweetened
> chocolate plus 1 Tbsp. sugar

Chocolate continued:

1 oz. square unsweetened chocolate = 3 Tbsp. cocoa powder plus 1 Tbsp. melted butter or margarine

4 ounce bar Baker's German Sweet Chocolate = ¼ cup Hershey's unsweetened cocoa powder, ¼ cup sugar & ¼ cup butter, margarine or shortening

6 ounces, semi-sweet chocolate = 2 ounces unsweetened chocolate, ½ cup sugar plus 2 Tbsp. butter

Coffee, 1 cup leftover brewed = 1 tsp. instant coffee powder plus ¾ cup boiling water; dissolved and cooled.

Crackers, ¾ crushed = 1 cup bread crumbs+

Eggs: 2 large eggs = 3 small eggs

 1 whole egg = 2 egg yolks (for custard)

 1 whole egg = 2 egg yolks plus 1 Tbsp. water (for cookies)

 2 whole eggs (for healthy substitutions) = 2 egg whites plus 1 whole egg

Marshmallow Creme, 7 oz. jar = 1, 16 ounce pkg. marshmallows, melted plus 3½ Tbsp. light corn syrup

Milk: 1 cup buttermilk = 1 Tbsp. vinegar or lemon juice plus sweet milk to equal 1 cup (let stand 10 minutes)

 1 cup whole milk = ½ cup evaporated milk plus ½ cup water

 1 cup skim milk = ¼ cup instant nonfat dry milk plus 1 cup water

Mustard, dry, 1 teaspoon = 1 Tbsp. prepared mustard

Sour cream, 1 cup = ⅔ cup milk plus ⅓ cup butter

Sour cream & plain non-fat yogurt are interchangeable

"Heavy cream" and "whipping cream" are the same

EQUIVALENT MEASUREMENTS:

Apples, 1 lb. = 2 large or 3 medium = 3 cups sliced

Bacon, ½ lb. cooked = ½ cup crumbled

Bananas, 1 lb. = 3 medium = about 1⅓ cups mashed or 2½ cups sliced

Bread, 1 slice = ½ cups soft crumbs

Cheese, 1 lb. = 4 cups, grated
Candied Fruits or Peels, ½ lb. = 1¼ cups, cut up
Carrots, shredded (for carrot cake) 1 lb. = 3 cups
Coconut, flaked: 3½ ounce can = 1⅓ cups
       7 ounce package = 2⅔ cups
       14 ounce package = 5⅓ cups
Coconut, grated, frozen = 6 oz. package = 1⅓ cups
Cranberries, raw, 1 lb. = 4 cups
Cream Cheese, 8 ounce package = 1 cup
Cream Cheese, 3 ounce package = 6 Tbsp.
CRUMBS: Saltine Crackers, 28 = 1 cup fine crumbs
       Chocolate Wafers, 19 = 1 cup crumbs
       Graham Crackers, 14 squares = 1 cup crumbs
         14.4-oz. box whole crackers = 4 cups crumbs
       Vanilla Wafers, 22 cookies = 1 cup fine crumbs
Dates, 1 lb. = 2 cups
Eggs, 1 whole egg = ¼ cup liquid
       4 to 5 whole eggs = 1 cup
       8 to 10 egg whites = 1 cup
       12 to 14 egg yolks = 1 cup
Grits, ¼ cup raw = 1 cup cooked
Lemons, 1 medium = 2 to 3 Tbsp. juice plus 2 tsp.
       grated rind
Limes, 1 medium = 1½ to 2 Tbsp. juice plus 1½ tsp.
       grated rind
Macaroni, Elbow, 2 cups uncooked = 4 cups cooked
Marshmallows, 10 large = 1 cup
       10 miniature = 1 large marshmallow
       8 ounce pkg. mini = 4½ cups
       10 ounce pkg. mini = 6 cups
       16 ounce pkg. mini = 9 cups
Milk, Evaporated, 5 oz. can = about ⅔ cup
       12 oz. can = about 1⅔ cups
       Sweetened Condensed, 14 ounce can = 1¼ cups
Nuts, Almonds, 1 lb. = 3½ cups shelled
       Peanuts, 1 lb. = 3 cups shelled
       Pecans, 1 lb. = 4 cups shelled

Oranges, 1 medium = ⅓ to ½ cup juice plus 2 to 3 Tbsp. grated rind

Orange Peel, dried, 1 Tbsp. = 2 to 3 Tbsp. fresh peel
2 tsp. dried = 1 tsp. orange extract

Raisins, 1 lb. = 2 cups, packed

Rice, Long grain, 1 cup uncooked = 3½ to 4 cups cooked, it depends on the brand

Sugar, Brown, 1 lb. box = 2⅓ cups
Powdered, 1 lb. box = 3½ cups
Granulated, 1 lb. = 2 cups

Unflavored Gelatin, ¼ ounce package = 1 Tbsp.

Vanilla, 1 vanilla bean = 1 tsp. vanilla extract
¼ tsp. powdered = 1 tsp. vanilla extract

Yeast, 1 cake compressed yeast = 1 package active dry yeast = ¼ oz. or 2¼ tsp.

Liquid & Dry Measurements

A "dash" = ¹⁄₁₆ teaspoon (about half of a "pinch")

A "pinch" = ⅛ teaspoon or as much as can be taken between tip of finger and thumb

3 teaspoons = 1 tablespoon or ½ ounce

⅛ cup = 2 tablespoons or 1 ounce

A "jigger" = 1½ ounces or 2½ tablespoons

¼ cup = 4 tablespoons or 2 ounces

⅓ cup = 5 tablespoons plus 1 teaspoon

½ cup = 8 tablespoons or 4 ounces

⅔ cup = 10 tablespoons plus 2 teaspoons

¾ cup = 12 tablespoons or 6 ounces

⅞ cup = 14 tablespoons or ¾ cup plus 2 tablespoons

1 cup = 16 tablespoons or 8 ounces

1 cup = ½ pint or 8 fluid ounces

2 cups = 1 pint or 16 ounces

4 cups = 2 pints or 1 quart or 32 ounces

2 pints = 1 quart

1 quart = 4 cups

2 quarts = ½ gallon

4 quarts = 1 gallon

8 quarts = 1 peck

4 **pecks** = 1 bushel
4 **tablespoons butter** = ¼ cup = 2 ounces = ½ stick
5⅓ **tablespoons butter** = ⅓ cup or ⅔ of a stick
6 **tablespoons butter** = ¾ of a stick
8 **tablespoons butter** = ½ cup *or* 4 ounces *or* 1 stick
½ **pint whipping cream** (1 cup) = 2 cups whipped
12 **large egg yolks** = about 1 cup
8 **large egg whites** = about 1 cup
5 **whole egg yolks** = 1 cup
¼ **cup egg substitute** = 1 whole large egg

*A*dditional measurements you just might need:
⅓ **of 2 tablespoons** = 2 teaspoons
½ **of 1 tablespoon** = 1½ teaspoons
⅓ **of ¼ cup** = 1 tablespoon plus teaspoon
⅓ **of ½ cup** = 2 tablespoons plus 2 teaspoons
⅓ **of ¾ cup** = ¼ cup
½ **of ⅓ cup** = 2 tablespoons plus 2 teaspoons
½ **of ¾ cup** = 6 tablespoons
½ **of 1¾ cup** = ¾ cup plus 2 tablespoons

Sometimes when Grandma gives you an old recipe, it will call for a certain "number" of the can rather than by the weight of the can. Here's the conversion:

Can Size (by number)	Weight	Cupfuls
#300	15 ounces	1¾ cups
#303	16 ounces	2 cups
#2	20 ounces	2½ cups
#2½	28 ounces	3½ cups
#3	33 ounces	4 cups
#10	106 ounces	13 cups

NOTE: Manufacturers will, from time to time, change the weight of their cans or add new ones. In that case, use the cupful measurements closest to what you're looking for. example: 28 oz. or 29 oz can, depends on the manufacturer.

BAKING DISH & PAN SIZE CONVERSIONS

Amount of batter: (²/₃ full)	Size of pan:
4 cups	8x2-inch round layer pan 9x1½-inch round layer pan 8½x4½x2½-inch loaf pan
6 cups	8x8x2¼-inch square pan 9x9x2-inch square pan 10x2-inch round cake pan 9x5x3-inch loaf pan 11x7x1½-inch rectangle pan
8 cups	15x10x1-inch jelly-roll pan
10 cups	9x3-inch Bundt cake pan 9x13x2-inch dish or pan
12 cups	10x4-inch Angel food tube pan

A recipe for two 8-inch layers will make *one* of these:

Cupcakes: 2½ dozen miniature size (1 inch)
2 dozen regular size (2¾ inch)
6 jumbo size (3½ inch)
Loaf Cake: (9x5x3 inch)
Oblong Cake: (9x13x2 inch)
Square: (two layers) (8x8x2 inch)

Springform: For cheesecakes

Size of pan:	Amt. of batter	# of servings
6x3-inch	4 cups	6-8
8x3-inch	12 cups	10-12
9x3-inch	16 cups	14-16
10x3-inch	20 cups	18-20

Pie Plates:

8x1¼-inch	4 cups
9x1¼-inch	5 cups
9x2-inch (deep dish)	8 cups
10x1½-inch	8 cups

Ring Molds:

8¼-inch	4 cups
9½-inch	6 cups
11-inch	8 cups (12 cups filled to the <u>top</u>)

Most casserole-type dishes call for 9x13x2, 9x9x2, or 8x8x2 inch baking dishes. But you might have a pretty round oven-proof baking dish you would want to use instead. When you visit the mountains, check out the handmade pottery shops where you can find some very beautiful 2 quart-size round oven-proof bowls.

Here's a guide for substitutions:

Size:	Size	Volume
1 quart casserole	9-inch square	4 cups
	9x5-inch loaf pan	
1½ quart casserole	9-inch square	6 cups
	9x5-inch loaf pan	
2 quart casserole	9x13x2-inch	8-12 cups

(Fill ½ full, for something that might boil over)
(You may fill to the top of the dish for foods like macaroni & cheese or lasagna, that won't spill over when baking)

2 quart round pyrex	8½x3-inch	7-8 cups

✪ven Temperatures:

Very slow oven	250 - 275 degrees
Slow oven	300 - 325 degrees
Moderate oven	350 - 375 degrees
Hot oven	400 - 425 degrees
Very hot oven	450 - 475 degrees
Extremely hot oven	500 - 525 degrees

Here we Come a-Wassailing

Hardly any of the multitude of gay and cheerful Christmas songs lends itself better to outdoor singing than this spirited carol. Wassailing, a centuries-old custom, gave an opportunity for groups of holiday revelers to offer a song and a hot drink from the Wassail Bowl in exchange for a gift.

TRADITIONAL

ENGLISH
Arranged by Ruth Heller

With spirit

1. ___ Here we come a-was-sail-ing A-mong the leaves so green; ___
2. We are not dai-ly beg-gars That beg from door to door; But
3. God bless the mas-ter of this house, Like-wise the mis-tress too; And
4. And all your kin and kins-folk That dwell both far and near, We

Here we come a-wan-d'ring, So fair___ to be seen.
we are neigh-bors' chil-dren, Whom you have seen be-fore.
all the lit-tle chil-dren, That round the ta-ble go.
wish a Mer-ry Christ-mas And Hap-py New-Year.

REFRAIN

Love and joy come to you, And to you your was-sail too; And God bless you and

send you a Hap-py New Year, And God send you a Hap-py New Year.

18

St. Nick's Nibbles, Bites & Nogs

RECIPES:

NIBBLES:

NOGS:

Smoky Cheeseball

2 8-oz. pkg. cream cheese, softened
1 8-oz. pkg. smoky cheddar cheese, shredded
½ cup butter, softened
2 Tbsp. milk
2 tsp. A-1 steak sauce
1 cup finely chopped pecans

Combine all ingredients, except pecans, in food processor or electric mixer and beat until fluffy. Chill slightly and shape into one (very) large ball or 2 medium-size balls. Roll in chopped pecans, coating it well.
NOTE: If you can't find smoky cheddar, use 2 or 3 drops of liquid smoke.

Cheese Pecan Wafers

2 cups (8-oz.) sharp Cheddar cheese, grated
1 cup butter, softened
2 cups flour
½ tsp. salt
Dash black pepper
2 cups Rice Krispie cereal
Pecan halves

Combine cheese and butter on *low* speed of electric mixer. Sift flour, salt & black pepper together and add to cheese mixture. Carefully stir in cereal. Chill 2 hours. Preheat oven to 350 degrees. Shape dough into one inch balls; place on *ungreased* cookie sheet and flatten with a fork. Top each wafer with a pecan half, pressing slightly into dough. Bake in preheated oven for 8 minutes. Makes about 6 dozen wafers.

PIMIENTO CHEESE

Good in stuffed celery hearts and great sandwiches!
My aunt Mae used to take these sandwiches to the
family get-togethers. She probably didn't use a recipe,
but this is very much like hers.

10 oz. sharp Cheddar cheese, grated
³/4 cup mayonnaise
1 4-oz. jar diced pimientos, undrained
4 drops Tabasco Sauce
½ tsp. garlic salt

Combine grated cheese and mayonnaise in food processor. Pulse several times till well mixed. Add undrained
pimientos, hot sauce and garlic salt. Process until
smooth. It will be runny, so chill at least one hour.
Makes 3 cups
NOTE: Be sure and use exactly 10 oz. If you use more,
it will be too hard and won't spread when it gets cold.
This is great pimiento cheese. The little bit of hot sauce
and garlic salt gives it a great taste.
VARIATION: Spread it on deli ham slices, roll up and cut
into one inch slices for an interesting addition to your
appetizer tray.

DILLY OF A DIP

1 cup sour cream
1 cup mayonnaise
1 tsp. dillweed

1 tsp. Beau Monde
1 tsp. dried parsley
1 tsp. dried onion flakes

Stir the sour cream and mayonnaise together. Add the
herbs, mixing well. Chill at least 2 hours to "mellow"
before serving with raw vegetables or chips.

Tex-Mex Dip

1 tsp. cumin
½ tsp. chili powder
¼ tsp. garlic salt
¼ tsp. onion powder
¼ tsp. paprika
1 cup dairy sour cream
1 cup mayonnaise

1 cup grated sharp cheese
1 4-oz. can chopped green
   chilies, drained

Combine spices. Add sour cream and mayonnaise, mixing well. Stir in cheese and chilies. Cover and refrigerate at least 2 hours.
Serve with Don Pablo's® restaurant-style round tortilla chips. They're uniformly round, nice & sturdy.

Becky's Chicken Bites

4-oz. cream cheese (½ of 8-oz. pkg.), softened
2 Tbsp. mayonnaise
1 cup cooked chicken, chopped
1 cup blanched almonds, chopped
1 Tbsp. prepared chutney, chopped
½ tsp. salt
1 tsp. curry powder
1 cup grated coconut, thawed

Combine softened cream cheese and mayonnaise. Add rest of ingredients *except* coconut. With hands, shape into small balls and roll in coconut.
Makes about 24 appetizers

CHICKEN NUGGETS

2 chicken breast fillets
¼ cup buttermilk
¼ cup self-rising flour
Salt & black pepper
Vegetable oil to fry

Rinse chicken and pat dry. Cut into bite-sized pieces.
Dip each piece in buttermilk and roll in mixture of flour,
salt and pepper. Place on wire rack and let stand until
coating is dry. Then roll again in remaining flour. Heat oil,
about 3 inches deep, to 350 degrees and fry chicken till
golden brown. Drain on paper towels and serve with
Honey Mustard Sauce.   Makes about 12 pieces

HONEY MUSTARD SAUCE

½ cup honey
¼ cup Dijon mustard
1½ cups mayonnaise

Whisk the three ingredients together until well blended
and serve with chicken nuggets.

Granny's Mini Recipes

1. Bake tiny red potatoes, cut in half *or* cut ⅓ of the
     top off, fluff with a fork and top with sour cream
   and chives.
2. Stir a little fresh basil into softened cream cheese,
     stuff into scooped out cherry tomatoes.
3. Scoop out some of the center of the cherry toma-
     toes and stuff with crabmeat.

SPINACH SQUARES

10 oz. pkg. frozen chopped spinach, thawed
2 Tbsp. butter
2 large eggs
½ cup all-purpose flour
1 tsp. baking powder
½ cup milk
1½ tsp. salt
White pepper to taste
1 8-oz. pkg. Monterey Jack Cheese, shredded

Preheat oven to 350 degrees. Melt butter in a 8" or 9" square baking dish. Take the spinach out of the package and place in a colander. When it is completely thawed, take a small plate or bowl and press down real hard, pushing out all of the water. In a large bowl beat the eggs lightly; add flour, baking powder, milk, salt, pepper, cheese and spinach, mixing well. Pour in prepared baking dish and bake for 35 minutes. Cut into small squares and serve immediately.
Makes 16 appetizer-size squares.
NOTE: This recipe can be doubled and baked in a 9x13-inch baking dish.

CRABBY CRACKERS

1¼ cups mayonnaise
1½ tsp. prepared horseradish
¼ cup French Dressing
¾ cup sharp Cheddar cheese, shredded
1½ cups fresh crabmeat (or 2, 6-oz. cans, drained and picked over for bits of shell)

Mix all together and serve with assortment of crackers.

Sausage Balls

This recipe has been around for a long time but it's nice to have it handy.

1 lb. bulk sausage, hot or mild, uncooked
2 cups Bisquick baking mix
1 cup sharp Cheddar cheese, shredded

Preheat oven to 350 degrees. Mix all three ingredients together with hands and form into one inch balls. Place on cookie sheet and bake for 25 minutes. Serve hot.
Makes about 70
NOTE: These can be made ahead and frozen, uncooked, until ready to use. Thaw before baking.
VARIATION: If you don't like hot sausage, use mild and add a drop or two of Tabasco Sauce or Texas Pete.

Broiled Shrimp

12 slices bacon
Dijon mustard

36 large shrimp, peeled & de-veined

Cut bacon in thirds. Spread mustard on each piece. Wrap around a shrimp and secure with a toothpick. Place on a cookie sheet and broil about 6 inches from broiler, turning once, for about 5 minutes on each side. Serve hot.   Makes 36 appetizers

Granny's Instant Dip

1 cup sour cream
1 cup creamy cottage cheese

1 envelope Italian salad dressing mix

Mix all together and serve with chips or celery sticks.

Celery Hearts With Blue Cheese Dip

This is the quickest & easiest appetizer when you need something fast!

1 pkg. celery hearts
1 8-oz. carton (1 cup) dairy sour cream
1 cup mayonnaise
1 4-oz. pkg. crumbled dairy blue cheese

Cut off tops and about one inch off the wide base. Separate and wash stalks. Cut each stalk into thirds. Blend sour cream and mayonnaise together with a spoon. Add crumbled blue cheese and mix well.
Put dip in a pretty little bowl or crock and surround with celery sticks. Makes 2 cups of dip *Men love these!*
NOTE: There are 2 stalks of celery ribs per package, so if you plan to use the whole package, you might want to double the dip recipe *or* save the 2nd one for another use.

Pineapple Stuffed Celery

1 3-oz. cream cheese, softened
3 Tbsp. mayonnaise
½ cup chopped pecans
½ cup crushed pineapple, well drained

Blend cream cheese and mayonnaise together.
Add pecans and crushed pineapple.
Fill 3-inch pieces of celery with mixture.
NOTE: If you don't care for pineapple, Soften 2, 8-oz. pkg. cream cheese, and add 1 cup chopped pecans or walnuts, eliminating the pineapple..

Granny Says:

The best way to keep kids at home is to make a pleasant atmosphere...and let the air out of their tires!

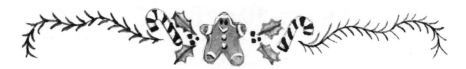

CHEDDAR BISCUITS
Very much like the ones served at one of your favorite restaurants.

2 cups Bisquick
³/₄ cup sharp cheddar cheese, grated
½ cup water
½ stick butter (¼ cup)
¼ tsp. garlic powder
1 tsp. dried parsley flakes
½ tsp. McCormick Italian Seasoning

Preheat oven to 450 degrees. Combine Bisquick, cheese and water. Drop by heaping tablespoonfuls onto an ungreased cookie sheet. Bake for 8 to 10 minuet. Meanwhile melt butter and add garlic salt, parsley and Italian seasoning. After baking, while still hot, brush butter mixture on top of biscuits.
Serve hot. Makes about 1 dozen.

MUSTARD SAUCE
Good to serve with ham biscuits or boiled shrimp.

1½ cups mayonnaise
½ cup Creole-style prepared mustard
1 Tbsp. prepared horseradish
2 Tbsp. lemon juice
Mix all of the above ingredients together.

TIP: Buy party-sized croissants or pkg. of little 1x2-inch brown & serve rolls, fill with slivers of ham.

SEAFOOD DIP

1 8-oz. container sour cream
1 envelope (1-oz.) packet Original Ranch Dip Mix
2 Tbsp. minced green onions
³/₄ cup desired seafood (crabmeat, tiny shrimp, etc.)

Combine sour cream, dip mix and green onions.
Fold in seafood. If using canned, drain well. Serve with
vegetables, sturdy chips or vegetable chips. The vegetable chips are really nice with this dip. Most major
grocery stores sell them. The chips are very colorful and
are made from vegetable slices.

SPINACH-CRABMEAT DIP

1 10-oz. pkg. frozen chopped spinach
1   6½ oz. can crabmeat, drained & picked over for bits
       of shell
1 cup mayonnaise
1 cup sour cream
Juice of 1 lemon (2 or 3 Tbsp.)
½ cup sliced green onions
1 Tbsp. chopped parsley
1 tsp. dried dill weed
1 tsp. salt

Thaw spinach. Place in a colander, putting a small plate
on top and squeeze out all of the liquid. Combine with
rest of the ingredients, mixing well. Chill for several
hours. Serve with raw veggies or crackers.
Makes 2 cups

Mrs. G's Oyster Crackers

1 cup vegetable oil
1 1-oz. envelope Ranch Salad Dressing Mix
½ Tbsp. dill weed
½ tsp. garlic powder
2 8-oz. boxes plain oyster crackers

Preheat oven to 275 degrees. Whisk the first 5 ingredients together and pour over oyster crackers, stirring well to coat. Place on baking sheets or in a large roasting pan and bake for 15 to 20 minutes Stir half way through. Cool and store in airtight container.
ALTERNATIVE METHOD OF PREPARING INSTEAD OF BAKING: After mixing the crackers with the oil mixture, put them in a gallon-size plastic bag, turning every once in a while. The crackers will absorb the liquid after 24 hours and won't be oily.

Cheesy Potato Skins

4 baking potatoes, baked
¼ cup dairy sour cream
1 1-oz. envelope Ranch Salad Dressing Mix
Sharp Cheddar Cheese, shredded

Preheat oven to 375 degrees. After the potatoes have cooled enough for you to handle, quarter them. Carefully scoop out most of the potato flesh, leaving about ¼ inch the potato and the shells in tact. Mash with the sour cream and dry dressing mix and fill the shells, making a nice rounded top. Sprinkle with shredded cheese and bake 12 to 15 minutes.
NOTE: For average size potatoes, bake for one hour. And for large potatoes bake 1½ hours.

SPINACH & ARTICHOKE DIP
Simple, easy & delicious dip.

1 16-oz container dairy sour cream (2 cups)
1 cup mayonnaise
1 1.4-oz. pkg. Knorr vegetable soup, dip & recipe mix*
1 Tbsp. dry onion soup mix
1 10-oz. pkg. frozen chopped spinach, thawed and
    squeezed dry
1 14-oz can artichoke hearts, drained and finely
    chopped

Mix sour cream, mayonnaise, vegetable soup mix and onion soup mix together. Add spinach and artichoke hearts, stirring until well blended. Chill for 2 hours before serving. Serve with toasted baguette slices. NOTE: Drained artichoke hearts can be chopped in food processor by pulsing a few times..
*NOTE: You can use one 1.8 oz. pkg. Lipton's Vegetable Recipe Soup & Dip Mix.
VARIATION: For extra flavor use 2, 6½ oz. jars of marinated artichoke hearts instead of canned.

SOUTHERN FRIED OKRA
"Finger food"?.... Mrs. Fred Hamilton told me to serve this as an appetizer. What a great idea!

2 lbs. fresh okra pods
1 cup all-purpose flour
½ cup yellow cornmeal
¼ tsp. cayenne pepper
2 tsp. Jane's Crazy
    Mixed-up Salt

Select small tender pods of whole okra and cut into ½ inch round slices; rinse & pat dry. Combine dry ingredients and coat okra, shaking off excess. Heat oil in heavy skillet or Dutch oven, filling ½ full to 350 degrees. Fry about 5 minutes till golden brown. Drain on paper towels. Serve immediately so they will be hot and crispy.

DIANNE'S PEPPER JELLY

3 large bell peppers (1¾ cups)
¼ cup jalapeno peppers, fresh or canned
4 cups granulated sugar
¾ cup apple cider vinegar
2 3-oz. pkg. liquid pectin
Optional: a few drops of food coloring

Puree bell peppers. in the food processor and measure out 1¾ cups. Puree seeded Jalapeno peppers. (wear rubber gloves and hold your breath, these are very hot and take your breath away) Measure out ¼ cup. Put the canning jars and lids on the stove in boiling water. Turn off stove and keep them in the hot water while you prepare the jelly.

I use a very large glass micro-wavable bowL for this next step: Combine the sugar, vinegar and pureed peppers. Mix well. Cover the bowl with waxed paper and microwave on 100%. After it comes to a rolling boil, time it for exactly 12 minutes, stirring twice.

Remove waxed paper and boil on 50% power for 3 minutes. Then add the 2 packages of pectin. Boil on high for *exactly* 2 minutes. Skim off foam.

Pour into the hot jars, wipe the rims with a cloth and close tightly. It should make about five 8-oz. jars. Set somewhere to cool. You should hear the popping sound of them sealing.

TO MAKE THIS ON TOP OF THE STOVE: Combine everything except the pectin in a very large pot. Bring to a rolling boil and boil on medium high for 5 minutes. Add the pectic and bring back to a boil and boil on medium high for 1 more minute. Pour in to hot jars immediately. NOTE: I use a combination of red & green bell peppers for Christmas. Also, I don't strain my pepper jelly. I like the tiny bits of pepper in it.

Cocktail Meatballs

1 lb. ground beef (chuck)
½ lb. ground pork
½ lb. ground veal
1 envelope dry onion soup mix
1 large egg
2 tsp. Accent
¼ cup dried bread crumbs
1 Tbsp. margarine
2 14-oz. bottles catsup
1 10-oz. jar current jelly

Combine meats, dry soup mix, egg, Accent and bread crumbs. Form into small meatballs. Brown in margarine. Mix catsup and jelly in crockpot or electric skillet. Cook in the sauce till done, then turn on low and serve with cocktail toothpicks.   Makes about 30 servings

VARIATION: Another good sauce combination is a 10-oz jar of grape jelly, 12-oz. bottle chili sauce and 1 tsp. Dijon mustard.

Jezebel Sauce

1 10-oz. jar pineapple preserves
1 5-oz. jar prepared horseradish
1 10-oz. jar apple jelly
1 6-oz. jar prepared mustard

Combine all of the above and spread over an 8-ounce block of softened cream cheese. Serve with assorted crackers.

TOASTED PECANS

⅓ cup butter-flavored Crisco, melted
1 Tbsp. Worcestershire sauce
½ tsp. Tabasco sauce or Texas Pete, or to taste
¼ tsp. black pepper
1 tsp. salt
1 lb. pecan halves (about 4½ cups)

Preheat oven to 300 degrees. Combine the first 5 ingredients together in a small bowl, mixing well so the spices don't "clump" up during baking. Put the pecan halves in a big bowl and pour the liquid mixture over them, stirring well to coat all of the pieces. Spread the nuts evenly in a shallow baking pan and bake 20 minutes, stirring often, especially around the sides of the pan, to keep them from burning. Spread in a single layer on paper towels to cool completely . Store in airtight container.
Makes 4 cups.

TOASTED PECANS #2

¼ cup butter
1½ tsp. ground cumin
¼ tsp. ground red pepper

3 cups pecan halves
2 Tbsp. sugar
1 tsp. salt

Preheat oven to 300 degrees. Combine butter, cumin and red pepper in a large saucepan. When butter melts, cook on medium, stirring constantly, for one minute. Remove from heat, add pecans, sugar and salt. Stir to coat well. Spread in a single layer in 15x10-inch jelly roll pan and bake for 20 minutes, stirring occasionally. Cool completely on paper towels. Store in airtight container.
Makes 3 cups.

PARTY CREAM PUFFS

1 cup water	1 cup all-purpose flour
½ cup butter	4 large eggs
¼ tsp. salt	

1. Bring water to a boil in a 2-qt. saucepan; Add butter and melt.

2. Just as soon as butter is melted, add flour and salt all at once and beat vigorously with a wooden spoon until mixture leaves the sides of the pan and forms a smooth ball. This takes about one minute.

3. Remove from heat; cool about 1 minute. With electric beaters on low speed, add eggs, one at a time. Then on high speed, beat dough vigorously until dough is smooth and shiny.

4. Line a baking sheet with parchment paper. Drop dough by a scant ¼ cupfuls and place onto the parchment paper about 2 inches apart.

5. Bake in a preheated 400 degree oven for 30 to 35 minutes, until golden brown.

Turn oven off, crack the oven door and allow puffs to cool. Cut off ⅓ of the top of each one and using a fork, remove any soft dough inside. Fill with desired pudding filling, replace tops and dust generously with powdered sugar or drizzle with chocolate icing.

While cream puffs are baking, make the filling with your favorite pudding mix, whipped cream or ice cream.

This makes 12 regular size cream puffs.

NOTE: For mini appetizer size, drop by rounded tea-spoonfuls onto parchment and bake at 400 degrees for about 18 minutes. Remove from baking sheet and place on cooling rack. Cool. Just before serving, cut off tops and fill with chicken salad, ham salad, favorite seafood recipe using crabmeat, tuna or shrimp,

Makes 40 to 50 appetizer size cream puffs.

Fill *just* before serving so they won't get soggy.

Party Sandwich Filling

1   8-oz. pkg. cream cheese, softened
¾ cup chopped pecans
¼ cup chopped bell pepper
¼ cup chopped onions
3 Tbsp. chopped pimiento
1 Tbsp. catsup
3 hard-cooked eggs, finely chopped
¾ tsp salt
Dash white pepper

Combine all ingredients. Remove crusts from bread.
Using Christmas cookie cutters, bell, tree, etc. cut bread
shape out and spread with sandwich filling. This also
makes good finger sandwiches, by cutting into 3 "fingers" after removing crusts and filling .

Chili Cheese Squares

½ lb. ground beef
6 large eggs, beaten
2 4-oz. cans chopped green chilies, drained
1 lb. sharp Cheddar cheese, grated
1 medium onion, finely chopped

Preheat oven to 350 degrees. Brown meat and drain
well. Mix all ingredients together and pour into a
greased 9x13-inch baking dish. Bake for 45 minutes.
Cut into one inch squares and serve hot.
Makes 40 squares

Granny's Tip:
Hollow out big green and red bell peppers and
fill with your favorite dips.

Hot Christmas Punch

1 6-oz. can frozen orange juice concentrate
1 6-oz. can frozen lemonade concentrate
1 pt. cranberry juice
1 qt. apple cider
1 medium bottle maraschino cherries, drained and juice
    reserved
2 cups sugar
2 cups water

In a large bowl, mix together the orange juice concentrate, lemonade concentrate, cranberry juice, apple juice and the reserved cherry juice. Using one of the juice cans, add 5 cans of water.

In a 4-qt. saucepan, combine the sugar and 2 cups of water and boil until syrupy, about 5 minutes. Add the juice mixture to the pan and re-heat to serve hot.

To serve: place a cherry in each serving cup and pour in warm punch. Makes about 16, 6-oz. servings

Hot Buttered Rum

½ cup light rum
3 cups apple cider
1 Tbsp. plus 1 tsp. light brown sugar
4 tsp. butter, divided
4 3-inch sticks cinnamon

Combine rum, cider and brown sugar in a saucepan. Bring to a boil, stir until sugar dissolves. Pour into 4 coffee size mugs and add one teaspoon butter and a cinnamon stick to each.

MULLED CIDER
At Halloween, this is called "Witches Brew"

2 qt. apple cider
½ cup orange juice
¼ cup lemon juice
2 Tbsp. sugar

2 tsp. whole cloves
1 tsp. ground nutmeg
Cinnamon sticks

Mix all ingredients together and bring just to a boil. Cool and strain. Serve hot with a cinnamon stick in each cup. Makes about 16 half-cup servings
NOTE: Cinnamon sticks are usually 3 inches long.

CHRISTMAS WASSAIL

1 gal. apple cider
1 qt. orange juice
1 cup fresh lemon juice
1 qt. pineapple juice

24 cloves
4 sticks cinnamon
1 cup light brown sugar
Cinnamon sticks for stirrers

Mix all ingredients in a very large saucepot and heat to the boiling point. Reduce heat and simmer on low for 45 minutes. Strain and serve in mugs with cinnamon sticks. Makes about 24, one cup servings
Serve with an assortment of holiday cookies.

EMERY'S FUZZY NAVEL

Fill: **8-oz glass about ¾ full of crushed ice.**
Add: **2 oz. of Peach Schnapps (¼ cup)**
Finish filling glass with: **fresh orange juice** and stir.
Makes 1 serving

Hot Spiced Cider

½ cup brown sugar
¼ tsp. salt
2 qt. apple cider
1 tsp. whole allspice

1 tsp. whole cloves
10 3-inch sticks of cinnamon
Dash of nutmeg

Combine brown sugar, salt and cider. Tie the spices in a piece of cheesecloth; add to cider mixture. Slowly bring to a boil; cover. Simmer for 20 minutes. Serve hot. Makes 10 servings

You can buy a package of 10 little draw-string bags at the kitchen shops, called "garni bags", to put the spices in. They can be washed and re-used.

To make little gift bags of cider spices:
Place one cinnamon stick, 2 whole cloves, 2 whole allspice and one tablespoon orange peel in each one of the little bags with the instructions to bring to a boil in a gallon of apple cider.

Glugg
A Swedish holiday drink

4 tsp. loose tea
1 qt. boiling water
2 3-inch cinnamon sticks
1 46-oz. can pineapple-grapefruit juice
1 pt. apple juice

Steep tea with the cinnamon sticks in the boiling water for 3 minutes, *Strain* the tea; add the fruit juices. Bring back to a boil. Serve hot. Store in refrigerator. Makes 20 servings.
NOTE: 46 ounces = 5 ¾ cups

HOT SPICED PERCOLATOR PUNCH

3 cups unsweetened pineapple juice
3 cups cranberry juice cocktail
1½ cups water
⅓ cup packed brown sugar
1½ tsp. whole cloves
1 Cinnamon stick, broken into pieces
⅛ tsp. salt

Combine first 4 ingredients together in percolator-type coffee maker. Place cloves, cinnamon stick and salt in percolator basket. Perk through full cycle. Serve hot.
Makes 10 servings
NOTE: For a 30 cup party percolator, multiply the above, times 3, and follow the same directions.
Great for a family get-together or holiday drop-ins to serve with Christmas cookies.

"But I *have* been good!"

40

Spiced Tea Punch

1   46-oz. can cran-apple juice
1   46-oz. can pineapple juice
1   46-oz. can orange juice
1   cup strong brewed tea
1   cup light brown sugar
2   tsp. whole cloves
3   6-inch cinnamon sticks

Pour juices and tea in 30 cup percolator. Put brown sugar, cloves and cinnamon sticks in the basket and perk through full cycle. Serve hot with tray of assorted Christmas cookies.
Suggestion: Lemon Bars or Pecan Tassies would be nice!

Make-Your-Own Wine Cooler

To make your own wine cooler, simply mix **equal parts of white wine and fruit juice**. For extra flavor, add some fruit flavored liqueur, to taste.

Packaging:

After mixing the following mixes, divide evenly among the desired number of gift jars.
The little wide mouth canning jars with the Holiday motif lids that are found in the canning section at the grocery store make a nice gift size for these instant mixes.
Just tie a red or green fat yarn around the top.
Punch a hole in a small gift card, put a little piece of jute through the hole and tie it to the yarn with hand-written instructions for it's use.

Sleighride Mocha Coffee Mix

Bundle up and drink this in insulated coffee mugs and munch on Christmas cookies. I can hear the sleigh bells and Christmas carols now!

2 cups cocoa powder
1 cup instant coffee crystals
2 cups coffee creamer
1½ cups sugar

1 tsp. cinnamon
¼ tsp. nutmeg
¼ tsp. salt

Mix all together in a large bowl and use 3 teaspoons of mix to 1 cup boiling water. If making in larger "traveling" mugs, double.

Instant Russian Tea Mix

A Miss Dee's Kitchen best seller!

1½ cups instant tea, sweetened & with lemon
1 cup pineapple/orange flavored Tang
1¾ cups sugar
½ tsp. each cinnamon and cloves

Mix all together and keep in an airtight container. To serve, add 3 to 4 teaspoons to ¾ cup boiling water for a 6-oz. cup.

NOTE: The Tang container holds exactly 3 cups, so by multiplying this recipe, times 3, and mixing in a large food processor, you get 3 gift jars.

Granny's Mini Recipe

Buy large cucumbers, slice into rounds.
Serve with a small mound of spinach dip on top.

Hot Chocolate Mix

5½ cups non-fat dry milk powder
¾ cup coffee creamer, plain or flavored
2½ cups cocoa powder
3 Tbsp. ground cinnamon
2 cups mini-marshmallows

Mix the dry milk powder, creamer, cocoa powder and cinnamon together. Stir in marshmallows. Makes 8½ cups of mix.
DIRECTIONS FOR SINGLE SERVING: Combine ⅓ cup of mix with 1 cup boiling water in coffee mug and stir to dissolve.

Holiday Hot Chocolate Mix

1 8-oz. box non-fat dry milk powder
1 3-lb. can NesQuik
1 1-lb. box sifted powdered sugar
1 6-oz. jar coffee creamer, plain or flavored

Mix all together. Divide evenly in gift containers.
DIRECTIONS FOR SINGLE SERVING: Use ¼ cup of mix with 1 cup boiling water.

Stuffed Pecans

Roquefort cheese   Jumbo pecan halves
Lemon juice or cream

Blend cheese into a smooth paste, moisten with several drops of lemon juice. Spread mixture on pecan halves, press halves together. Couldn't be easier! For extra zest, you may roast the pecans first, see page 34

Jolly Old Saint Nicholas

Anonymous

Anonymous

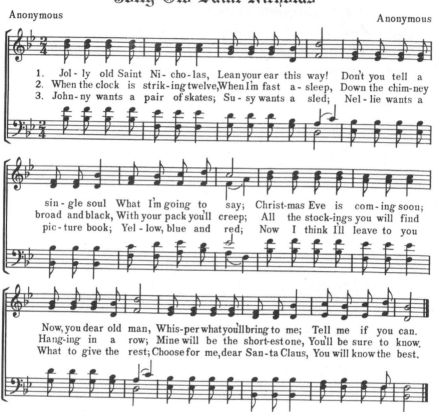

1. Jol - ly old Saint Ni - cho - las, Lean your ear this way! Don't you tell a
2. When the clock is strik-ing twelve, When I'm fast a - sleep, Down the chim-ney
3. John-ny wants a pair of skates; Su - sy wants a sled; Nel - lie wants a

sin - gle soul What I'm going to say; Christ-mas Eve is com-ing soon;
broad and black, With your pack you'll creep; All the stock-ings you will find
pic - ture book; Yel - low, blue and red; Now I think I'll leave to you

Now, you dear old man, Whis-per what you'll bring to me; Tell me if you can.
Hang-ing in a row; Mine will be the short-est one, You'll be sure to know.
What to give the rest; Choose for me, dear San-ta Claus, You will know the best.

©1995 Delafield Stamp Company

Mrs. Kringle's Candy

RECIPES:

Extras:

Candy Syrup Temperatures
Without a Thermometer

A ½ teaspoonful of syrup dropped into fresh cold water:

Thread: (230-232 degrees)	Spins a soft 2 inch thread when dropped from a spoon
Soft Ball (234-240 degrees)	Forms a ball when pressed together but does not hold it's shape
Firm Ball (242-248 degrees)	Forms a ball that holds it's shape
Hard Ball (250-268 degrees)	Forms a hard, but plastic ball
Soft Crack (270-290 degrees)	Forms hard, but not brittle thread
Hard Crack (300-310 degrees)	Forms hard, brittle thread that breaks when pressed

NOTE: Granny recommends investing in a candy thermometer if you're going to make candy very often or even just at Christmas-time. It will make your life a whole lot easier. It takes the guesswork out of candy making and makes you more confident.

Some of the more common types of candy that would call for the above temperatures are:

Soft Ball: fudge, pralines, fondants,
Firm Ball: caramels
Hard Ball: divinity, taffy & caramel corn
Soft Crack: toffee, butterscotch
Hard Crack: peanut and pecan brittles

CANDY TIPS

1. When cooking candy, choose the right size pan to cook it in. It should be large enough to let the candy boil freely without running over...heavy enough to eliminate burning..and have a tight fitted lid to put on for "curing" the first few minutes, if called for.

2. Milk scorches easily. Cook over medium heat. Candy containing water can be cooked much faster because there is no danger of scorching.

3. Watch candy closely during the last few minutes of cooking. There will be a quicker rise in temperature after it reaches 220 degrees.

4. Make candy on a clear, dry day. Candy picks up moisture from the air (especially divinity). If you do make candy on a rainy day, cook it at a temperature 2 degrees higher than called for in recipe.

5. Stir candy with a wooden spoon. Switch to a heavier spoon when the time comes to beat the mixture.

6. Do not reuse stirring spoon once mixture has begun to cook. Use clean spoon each time you remove mixture to test in cold water.

7. When a recipe calls for butter or margarine, use it to grease sides of saucepan before adding the other ingredients.

8. Use light brown sugar in recipes calling for brown sugar unless otherwise specified. Candy will have a lighter and more delicate flavor.

9. Add butter to candy as soon as it is removed from heat unless otherwise specified.

11. Measure ingredients carefully.

12. Use candy thermometer, if possible. Be sure bulb of thermometer is immersed and not resting on bottom of pan. Read thermometer at eye level.

13. Store all candies in tightly closed containers.

14. Dip gift candies in prepared chocolate coating. One pound of chocolate (purchased from candy-making suppliers or local candy-makers) will cover 70 to 80 candy centers.

How To Make Perfect-Every-Time Fudge

1. Select pans with high, smooth sides

2. Butter sides of pan well. This will keep sugar crystals from forming.

3. Stir constantly until it reaches boiling point. Make sure all sugar crystals have dissolved.

4. Place candy thermometer on side of pan Don't let *bulb* touch the bottom of the pan. Cook until candy reaches 234 degrees. Watch closely, once thermometer reaches 220 degrees, it will climb fast from there.

5. Cool to 110 degrees before beating. Remove pan from stove and place in cold water, leaving thermometer in place. Do not jar pan. Add butter to top, but <u>do</u> <u>not</u> <u>stir</u> <u>in.</u>

6. When candy has reached 110 degrees, start beating with a wooden spoon. Beat vigorously until candy stiffens and loses it's gloss. Don't stop too soon!

7. Push candy from pan with spatula onto a buttered dish. <u>Don't scrape pan.</u> If fudge doesn't set, it was not beaten long enough or was not cooked enough. To save it, add ¼ cup milk, stir, re-cook, beat, pour out.

About Paraffin Wax:

   Paraffin wax is consumable wax, used with chocolate to coat many candies. It can be found in the cake supply section in craft stores and the canning supply section of grocery stores.

   Paraffin wax comes in a 1-lb. box with 4 blocks.   If a recipe calls for ¼ lb. use one block. If it calls for ½ block, cut one of these blocks in half with a sharp knife. They're usually melted with the chocolate in top of a double boiler.

MOTHER'S OLD FASHIONED COCOA FUDGE

In the 1940's my mother made this candy every Saturday night. Mother, my dad & I would play cards, eat fudge and listen to "Your Hit Parade" on the radio.

2 cups granulated sugar
½ cup unsweetened Hershey's cocoa powder
1 Tbsp. light corn syrup
1 cup milk
1 tsp. vanilla
⅓ cup sweet butter
1 cup chopped walnuts or pecans

Combine sugar, cocoa, corn syrup, and milk in a saucepan. Bring to a boil, stirring constantly. Cook without stirring to 234 degrees on a candy thermometer, or until a small amount dropped into cold water forms a soft ball. Remove from heat and add vanilla, butter and nuts. DO NOT STIR. Cool 30 to 35 minutes. Beat with a wooden spoon until fudge thickens and loses some of it's gloss. Spread on a buttered platter or foil lined 8-inch square pan. Cool. If using foil, lift fudge out of pan. Cut into small squares. Store in an airtight container in a cool dry place.

NOTE: Mother always poured her fudge out on a buttered platter.

Dianne with Dad & Mother, 1936

Buttermilk Fudge

1 tsp. baking soda
1 cup buttermilk
2 cups granulated sugar
3 Tbsp. light corn syrup
1 tsp. vanilla
1 cup chopped pecans or walnuts

Add baking soda to buttermilk and let stand at least 5 minutes. Add sugar and corn syrup. Place in large saucepan and cook to the soft ball stage. Remove from heat. Cool to lukewarm. Add vanilla and nuts. Beat with wooden spoon till mixture begins to thicken, loses it's glossy appearance and holds its shape. Pour onto a buttered platter or into a buttered 8-inch square pan. Cool completely and then cut into squares.
Makes 1 pound.

VARIATION: Instead of pouring in pan, drop by teaspoonfuls onto a buttered cookie sheet.
VARIATION: Add ½ cup coconut instead of nuts.
VARIATION: This recipe doubles very easily. You might want to add pecans to one half and coconut to the other half.

White Peanut Butter Fudge

1 16 oz. pkg. white chocolate chips
1 12-oz. jar crunchy peanut butter

Melt chocolate chips and stir in peanut butter. Pour into a buttered 8-inch square or 11x7x1½-inch pan. Refrigerate until firm. Cut into small squares.

Chocolate-Peanut Butter Fudge

2 cups sugar
2 Tbsp. cocoa powder
2 Tbsp. cornstarch
⅓ cup light corn syrup
½ cup evaporated milk

1 Tbsp. butter
1 tsp. vanilla
⅓ cup peanut butter

Combine sugar, cocoa, cornstarch, syrup and milk in a large saucepan; cook over low heat until mixture is soft-ball stage. (234 degrees) Remove from heat; add butter and vanilla. Cool to lukewarm. Beat until almost hard. Add peanut butter. Pour into buttered plate. VARIATION: You may use creamy or crunchy peanut butter, your choice. Also ½ cup chopped peanuts could be added with creamy peanut butter.

Never-fail Peanut Butter Fudge

2 cups sugar
⅔ cup milk
1 cup peanut butter

1 cup marshmallow creme
1 tsp. vanilla

Combine sugar and milk in medium saucepan; cook to soft-ball stage Remove from heat; add peanut butter, marshmallow creme (be sure and add only 1 cup) and vanilla. Stir well. Pour into a buttered 9-inch square pan. When set, cut into small squares.

NOTE: 1 cup marshmallow creme is ½ of a 7 ounce jar.

Granny Says:
How come a 2-pound box of candy can
make you gain 5 pounds?

Mamie Eisenhower's Million Dollar Fudge

This recipe first came out in the early 1950's, named after a popular First Lady. This recipe makes a lot and you really need to make it during the holidays. Read the whole recipe, including the note at the bottom before starting.

Get everything ready before you start!!

SYRUP:
4½ cups sugar   2 Tbsp. butter
⅛ teaspoon salt   1 12-oz. can evaporated milk

CHOCOLATE MIXTURE:
1 12-oz. pkg. chocolate chips (2 cups)
3 4-oz. bars German Sweet Chocolate, broken up
7 oz. jar marshmallow creme (about 2 cups)

ADD LAST:
2 cups chopped pecans

Spray a 15x10-inch jelly roll pan with cooking spray and set aside.

Put the 2 chocolates and marshmallow creme in a very large bowl. Have the pecans ready to add last.

Put the sugar, salt, butter and evaporated milk in a large heavy saucepan. Over medium heat, bring to a boil; boil for exactly 6 minutes, without stirring (time this). Pour the boiling syrup over the chocolate mixture; beat until chocolate is completely melted. Stir in the pecans. Pour fudge into pan and spread evenly. Let cool till firm at room temperature a few hours before cutting into desired squares. Store in an airtight container.
Makes about 4 pounds.
NOTE: When the syrup starts a rolling boil, it will boil up to the top of your pan, so watch it. Also putting a little wire under your pan will protect your boiling process.

Milk Chocolate Truffles

1½ lb. milk chocolate, shaved or finely chopped
⅓ cup whipping cream
⅓ cup half-and-half
½ tsp. vanilla
Chocolate coating for dipping

Melt chocolate in top of double boiler over hot (not boiling) water. When melted, stir until smooth. Combine cream and half-and-half in a small saucepan; heat to scalding. (see below)

Remove from heat and let stand until temperature is about 130 degrees. Add the warm cream to melted chocolate all at once. Beat until smooth and well blended. Remove from heat; add vanilla and let cool.

When cool, beat with electric mixer until candy is light and fluffy. Place in refrigerator until firm.

When firm, roll a teaspoonful of candy into a ball with palm of hands. Roll each ball immediately into chocolate coating of your choice.
Makes 2 pounds or about 36 to 40 truffles.
Store truffles in refrigerator.

VARIATIONS:
#1: Substitute semi-sweet or dark chocolate
#2: Add 2 teaspoons Kahlua, coffee liqueur, with vanilla.
#3: Add 2 teaspoons Praline liqueur with vanilla and roll in toasted pecans, finely chopped after toasting.
#4: Add 2 teaspoons of Amaretto with vanilla and roll in toasted slivered almonds, finely ground.

Dear Granny: What do you mean by "scalding" the milk?
Answer: To heat to a temperature just below the boiling point. A thin skim forming over milk indicates sufficient heating.

Dianne's Toffee

½ cup butter
½ cup margarine
1¼ cups light brown sugar
¾ cup chopped pecans
1 6-oz. pkg. chocolate chips
Additional chopped nuts for top

Melt butter and margarine together over low heat; add brown sugar and nuts. Turn heat to high, stir quickly until color changes to light caramel, which takes 5 minutes. Remove from heat; pour in ungreased 9x13-inch pan, spreading evenly with a spatula. Drop chocolate chips evenly over hot candy, spread with a spatula. While still warm, score with pizza cutter. Top with additional nuts before it set up.
Makes 8 oz. of candy

Hershey's 1930's Fudge

3 cups sugar
⅔ cup Hershey's cocoa
⅛ tsp. salt

1½ cups milk
¼ cup butter
1 tsp. vanilla

Butter 8 or 9-inch square pan. Combine sugar, cocoa and salt in a heavy 4 quart saucepan; stir in milk. Cook over medium high heat, stirring constantly until mixture comes to a boil. Boil without stirring to soft-ball stage (234 degrees). Remove from heat; add butter and vanilla. DO NOT STIR. Cool at room temperature to 110 degrees. (lukewarm) Beat with wooden spoon until fudge thickens and just begins to lose some of it's gloss. Quickly spread into pan. Cut into small squares. VARIATION: Add 1 cup chopped pecans or walnuts

JERRY'S EASY PRALINES

1 lb. box light brown sugar
Pinch of salt
²⁄₃ cup (5-oz. can) evaporated milk
2 tsp. vanilla
2 cups pecan halves

Combine sugar, salt and milk in a saucepan. Place over low heat until sugar dissolves. Let mixture come to a rolling boil and cook, without stirring, for about 2 minutes (or 232 degrees on a candy thermometer). Remove from heat and add vanilla and nuts. Beat with a wooden spoon and drop by tablespoonfuls onto waxed paper. Work fast because it hardens quickly.
As soon as they are firm, remove from paper and place on serving plate. Makes about 2 dozen

KAHLUA PRALINES

1 cup granulated sugar	2 Tbsp. butter
1 cup packed brown sugar	2 tsp. vanilla
½ cup evaporated milk	3 Tbsp. Kahlua
⅛ tsp. salt	2 cups pecan halves

In a heavy saucepan, combine sugars, milk and salt. Cook over low heat, stirring constantly, until sugar dissolves. Increase heat to medium and bring to a boil. Cook until temperature reaches 234 degrees. Remove from heat; stir in butter, vanilla, Kahlua and pecans. Return to medium heat and cook until it reaches soft ball stage. Quickly drop by tablespoonfuls onto waxed paper. Cool and peel off paper.

Buttermilk Pecan Pralines

2 cups granulated sugar
1 cup buttermilk
1 tsp. baking soda
Pinch of salt

2 Tbsp. butter
1 tsp. vanilla
2½ cups pecan halves

In a large saucepan, combine sugar, buttermilk, baking soda and salt. Cook, stirring constantly, for 5 minutes. Add butter, vanilla and pecan halves. Cook 5 minutes more or until mixture reaches the soft-ball stage. Remove from heat and beat with wooden spoon until just creamy. Drop by tablespoonfuls onto lightly buttered waxed paper and allow to cool. Store in airtight container.

Rum Balls

1 cup vanilla wafer crumbs
1 cup powdered sugar
1½ cups chopped pecans or walnuts
2 Tbsp. unsweetened cocoa powder
2 Tbsp. light corn syrup
¼ cup rum
Powdered sugar to coat

Combine all of the above, mixing well. Shape into small balls and roll in powdered sugar. Let stand on waxed paper or cookie sheet to dry. Store in airtight container. Makes about 4 dozen.

Easy Caramel Corn

2 cups packed brown sugar
1 cup butter or margarine
½ cup light corn syrup
½ tsp. cream of tartar
1 tsp. baking soda
1 tsp. vanilla
4 qt. popped popcorn

Preheat oven to 250 degrees. Boil the first 4 ingredients for 5 minutes. Remove from heat and add baking soda and vanilla. It will foam. Put popped corn in a large turkey roaster or two 9x13-inch pans and pour hot syrup over it, mixing well. Bake for 1 hour, stirring often, about every 15 minutes. Cool and break apart.
NOTE: ½ cup raw popcorn will yield 4 quarts, popped.

Popcorn Crunch

8 cups popcorn, popped
1⅓ cups pecan halves
⅔ cup almonds
⅓ cup sugar

1 cup butter
½ cup light corn syrup
1 tsp. vanilla

Mix popcorn, pecans and almonds on cookie sheet. Combine sugar, butter and syrup in large heavy saucepan; bring to a boil over medium heat, stirring constantly. Continue boiling, stirring occasionally for 10 to 15 minutes or until mixture turns light caramel color. Remove from heat; stir in vanilla. Pour over popcorn mixture, mixing to coat well. Let cool. Break apart; store in tightly covered container.
Makes about 2 pounds

PECAN LOGS
Just like the ones sold at Cracker Barrel & Stuckey's

1 7-oz. jar marshmallow creme
1 16-oz. pkg. powdered sugar
1 tsp. vanilla
1 14-oz. pkg. caramels
3 Tbsp. water
1 to 1½ cups chopped pecans

Combine the first 3 ingredients, mixing well with hands. Shape into six 6X1 inch logs. Mixture will be very dry. Chill 2 to 3 hours. Combine caramels and 3 tablespoons water in top of a double boiler. Over simmering water, melt caramels, stirring frequently, till completely melted. Carefully dip logs in melted caramel and roll in chopped pecans. Chill 1 hour. Makes 6 rolls.
NOTE: They will be easier to dip if frozen first.
VARIATION: Roll in flaked coconut instead of pecans.

These make a nice addition to a party tray when you cut them into ½ or ¾ inch slices.

BUTTERSCOTCH ROUNDS

1 cup butterscotch morsels
⅓ cup sweetened condensed milk
1 tsp. vanilla
⅓ cup chopped pecans
Chopped pecans

Melt morsels in top of double boiler, stirring till smooth. Remove from heat and add sweetened condensed milk, vanilla and chopped pecans. Chill till firm.
Form into one long roll and roll into the extra chopped pecans, pressing pecans firmly into candy. Wrap in plastic wrap and refrigerate till firm. When ready to serve, cut into ½ inch slices. Makes about 24 slices

CHOCOLATE PEANUT BUTTER BALLS

1½ cups graham cracker crumbs
1½ cups flaked coconut
1½ cups chopped pecans
1 lb. box powdered sugar
1 12-oz. jar crunchy peanut butter
1 tsp. vanilla
1 cup butter or margarine, melted
½ bar paraffin
1 6-oz. pkg. semi-sweet chocolate chips

In a big bowl combine the first 7 ingredients together, mixing well. With hands, shape into small one inch balls. Freeze. Melt paraffin in top of double boiler. Add chocolate chips and stir until toughly melted. Using a long wooden skewer, carefully spear the balls, one at a time, and dip into the chocolate mixture, using a second skewer to remove and place on waxed paper to set up. Makes about 100
NOTE: Another nice tool to have in your "candy kitchen" is a candy dipping fork. (found in kitchen shops and Michael's)

MILLIONAIRES

1 14-oz. pkg. caramels
3 to 4 Tbsp. milk
2 cups chopped pecans

½ bar paraffin wax
1 12-oz. pkg. semi-sweet chocolate chips

Melt caramels in milk over low heat; add pecans. Drop by teaspoonfuls onto buttered waxed paper. Chill till firm. Melt paraffin and chocolate chips in top of double boiler over simmering water. Dip candy into chocolate, using a pointed toothpick. Place each on waxed paper. Chill.

Mother's Sugared Pecans

1 cup granulated sugar
¼ tsp. salt
½ tsp. cinnamon
1 tsp. grated orange rind

6 Tbsp. milk
1 tsp. vanilla
2 cups pecan halves

Combine sugar, salt, cinnamon and orange rind in a
saucepan. Stir in milk and cook to the soft ball stage,
stirring constantly, while cooking. Remove from heat;
add vanilla and pecans. Stir until "grainy". Turn out
immediately onto a buttered pan or plate and separate.
NOTE: Either use a candy thermometer, bringing to 232
to 240 degrees or drop about ½ teaspoon in a little
dish of cold water, pinching together with your fingers to
see if it holds together into a soft ball.

Reindeer Munchies

Every year I put a big bag of these in my out-of-town
Christmas packages . Better double recipe!

1 cup small pretzels
1 cup Apple-Cinnamon Cherrios cereal
1 cup graham cracker cereal
1 cup chopped pecans
1 12-oz. pkg. white chocolate chips

Combine pretzels, cereals and pecans in a large bowl.
Melt chocolate chips over low heat in a saucepan or in a
microwave proof dish on high for one minute, stirring
halfway through. Pour melted chocolate over mixture in
bowl, stirring well to coat. Spread out on waxed paper
lined cookie sheets. When completely cool, break into
large pieces and store in airtight containers.
Place in cellophane bags & tie with pretty ribbon or fat
red yarn. *Great munchies!!*

Aunt Judy's Molasses Candy
Also called "Old Fashioned Molasses Taffy"

1 cup sugar
2 cups molasses
½ cup water

1½ Tbsp. vinegar
½ tsp. baking soda
2 Tbsp. butter

Combine sugar, molasses, water and vinegar in a 3 quart heavy saucepan. Stir with a wooden spoon until sugar is dissolved. Cook to the hard ball stage (260 degrees on candy thermometer). Remove from heat and add soda and butter, stirring well. Pour out into a lightly oiled 9x13-inch pan (do not scrape cooking pan) and cool until it can be handled easily. Pull and stretch with lightly oiled fingers until it reaches a light color. Finally stretch into a long rope and cut into bite-size pieces with buttered scissors. When cold, wrap pieces individually in waxed paper, twisting paper ends.

Very Important: If you are testing the candy in cold water instead of using a candy thermometer, *do not* re-use stirring spoon once mixture has begun to cook. Use clean spoon each time you remove mixture to test in cold water.

Granny's Taffy Tips:

1: It's easier to cut the pieces if, after cutting the first piece, you turn the rope of taffy halfway over and cut another piece; continue cutting & turning.

2: Let the pieces fall separately onto a surface that has been buttered or dusted with powdered sugar and cool completely before wrapping in waxed paper.

3: Wrapping pieces of taffy individually in waxed paper makes them keep better, but they can be stored successfully unwrapped, in airtight containers in the refrigerator or freezer.

Rocky Road Squares

1 12-oz. pkg. chocolate chips
2 Tbsp. real butter
1 14-oz. can sweetened condensed milk
2 cups chopped pecans
1 10-oz. pkg. miniature marshmallows

Combine chocolate chips, butter and sweetened condensed milk in a saucepan over low heat. Stir until chips are melted. Remove from heat and cool slightly.
Put pecans and marshmallows in a large bowl and pour melted chocolate mixture over them, stirring very carefully to coat. You want to see fully formed marshmallows. Spread evenly in well greased 9x13-inch pan or pyrex dish. Chill for 2 hours until firm. Cut into small squares. Store covered at room temperature.

Ms. Noah's Easy Toffee
Taste like some famous little candy bars!

1 cup chopped pecans
½ cup butter
¾ cup light brown sugar, packed
4 plain Hershey Bars, (1.55-oz. size)

Butter an 8-inch square pan. Line pan with aluminum foil, extending over edges. Cover the bottom with the pecans. Melt butter and brown sugar together in a medium saucepan. Over medium heat boil for exactly 6 minutes, stirring constantly with a wooden spoon. Remove and pour over pecans; stir well. While still hot, lay the candy bars on top of warm candy; let sit 1 to 2 minutes and spread evenly to cover. Let cool completely. Then holding the foil, lift the candy out of the pan. Break into uneven pieces.

Macaroon Bon Bons

1 16-oz. pkg. powdered sugar
4 cups flaked coconut
2 cups finely chopped pecans
½ cup butter, melted
1 tsp. vanilla
⅔ cup sweetened condensed milk
White chocolate coating

Combine sugar, coconut and pecans. Stir in butter, vanilla and sweetened condensed milk (be sure and measure out ⅔ cup). Shape into small balls and freeze. Melt white coating chocolate in microwave and dip balls while still frozen.

Bon Bons

¼ cup lemon juice
¼ cup orange juice
1 Tbsp. grated lemon or orange rind
3 cups finely crushed vanilla wafers
2 Tbsp. unsweetened cocoa powder
1 cup powdered sugar
1 cup finely chopped pecans or walnuts
Granulated sugar to roll candy in

Combine all of the above, except granulated sugar, together in medium bowl. Form into small balls and roll in granulated sugar.

Granny Says:
"A recipe that is not shared with others will soon be forgotten. But when it's shared, it will be enjoyed by future generations."

PERFECT DIVINITY

2½ cups sugar
½ cup light corn syrup
½ cup hot water
¼ tsp. salt

2 large egg whites
1 tsp. vanilla
1 cup chopped pecans
Pecan halves

In a heavy 2-quart saucepan, over low heat, combine sugar, corn syrup, hot water and salt. Cook until sugar is dissolved. Continue cooking, without stirring till hardball (250 degrees), about 15 minutes.

Meanwhile beat egg whites until stiff peaks form.

Pour *half* of the hot syrup slowly over beaten egg whites in a thin stream, beating constantly at medium speed, about 5 minutes.

Cook remaining half of syrup over medium heat, stirring occasionally, until candy thermometer registers 272 degrees (about 4 or 5 minutes.

Slowly pour hot syrup and vanilla over egg whites, beating constantly until mixture hold shape when dropped from spoon. (about 6 to 8 minutes) Fold in chopped pecans.

Drop by rounded teaspoon, pushing off with a second spoon, onto lightly buttered foil or waxed paper.

Top each piece of candy with a pecan half, if desired. Makes about 24 pieces.

NOTE: Stir in a few drops of red food coloring to make pretty pink divinity. Aunt Judy used to make 2 batches, tinting one with red food coloring and the other one with green food color.

Strawberry Divinity Squares

3 cups sugar
³/₄ cup light corn syrup
³/₄ cup water
2 large egg whites
1 3-oz. pkg. strawberry Jell-O
½ cup chopped pecans (+ more for top)

Combine sugar, corn syrup and water in a large saucepan; bring to a boil, stirring constantly. Reduce heat. Cook, stirring constantly to hard-ball stage (250 degrees on candy thermometer). Beat egg whites until stiff peaks form; add Jello, beating well. Pour hot syrup into egg-white/Jell-O mixture in a *thin stream;* beat on high speed until mixture is no longer glossy and holds shape. Fold in ½ cup chopped pecans. Pour into greased 9-inch square pan. Top with additional coconut and pecans. Cool and cut into squares, 6 across & 6 down. Makes 36 pieces
NOTE: Insead of pouring candy into a pan, you can drop by spoonfuls on waxed paper.

Never-Fail Divinity

½ cup water
2 cups sugar
Pinch of salt
1 pt. jar marshmallow creme

1 tsp. vanilla
1 cup chopped pecans

Combine water, sugar and salt in large heavy saucepan, bringing to a boil. Boil to 250 degrees (hard-ball stage) Place marshmallow creme in a bowl; add boiling syrup, stirring until soft peaks form. Add vanilla and pecans, stir. Drop by spoonfuls onto buttered foil.

PECAN BUTTER CRUNCH

1 cup butter, melted
1⅓ cups granulated sugar
1 Tbsp. light corn syrup
3 Tbsp. water
1 cup coarsely chopped pecans
2 regular size plain Hershey Bars, melted
1 cup finely chopped pecans, divided

Melt butter in large saucepan. Add sugar, corn syrup and water. Cook, stirring constantly, to the hard crack stage, (330 degrees). Watch very closely. Quickly stir in coarsely chopped pecans. Spread on ungreased 9x13-inch baking pan. Cool thoroughly. Melt Hershey bars in top of double boiler. Turn candy out on waxed paper and spread with ½ of the melted chocolate; sprinkle with half the chopped pecans. Cover with waxed paper; invert and spread with the rest of the melted chocolate, sprinkling with remaining half pecans. Let dry several hours or overnight. Break into pieces.

COCONUT BALLS

½ cup butter, softened
2 1 lb. boxes powdered sugar
1 14-oz. can sweetened condensed milk
1 tsp. coconut or vanilla extract
1 14-oz. pkg. flaked coconut
1½ cups chopped pecans
1 12 oz. pkg. chocolate chips (white or semi-sweet)
½ bar paraffin wax

Continued

Continued:
Cream butter and sugar. Add condensed milk, extract, coconut and pecans. Mix well with hands, forming into 1-inch balls. Freeze. Melt paraffin wax and chocolate in top of double boiler, stirring well. Insert wooden pointed toothpick in balls and dip in melted chocolate mixture. Carefully pushing off with another wooden toothpick, place on waxed paper till set.

COCONUT- DATE BALLS

2 cups sugar
½ cup butter, melted
1 8-oz. pkg. chopped dates
1 large egg
1 tsp. vanilla

1 tsp. coconut extract
2 cups rice crispy cereal
1 cup chopped pecans
7-oz can flaked coconut

Combine sugar and butter in a large saucepan, stirring constantly until mixture comes to a boil. Add chopped dates. In a small dish, slightly beat the egg. Add a little of the hot mixture to the egg and then stir that into the saucepan. Cook on low heat for 10 minutes, stirring constantly. Let cool completely. Add extracts, cereal and pecans. Shape into small balls and roll in coconut. Makes about 4 dozen.

Over the river and through the wood,
with a clear blue winter sky,
The dogs do bark and the children hark,
as we go jigling by.
Lydia Maria Child (1802-1880)

Rudolph's Peanut Clusters

2 lbs. white chocolate coating
1 12-oz. pkg. semi-sweet chocolate chips
1 11½ oz. pkg. milk chocolate chips
1 16-oz. jar unsalted dry roasted peanuts

Melt chocolate coating and both kinds of chocolate chips in top of double boiler over simmering water. When melted, remove from heat and cool 5 minutes. Stir in peanuts and drop by tablespoonfuls onto waxed paper. Cool completely. Store in refrigerator.

Crunchy Cinnamon Pecan Crackers

12 cinnamon graham crackers
2 cups chopped pecans
1 cup light brown sugar, firmly packed
1 cup butter
½ tsp. cinnamon

Preheat oven to 350 degrees. Spray the bottom of a 15x10-inch jelly roll pan lightly with Pam. Arrange the graham crackers in a single layer with sides touching. Spread the nuts evenly over crackers. In a small saucepan, combine sugar, butter and cinnamon. Bring to a boil and boil for 2 minutes, stirring constantly. Spoon syrup evenly over nuts. Bake in preheated oven for 10 minutes. Cool completely, break into pieces and store in an airtight container.

A Christmas tin full of these makes a nice gift.

TRACEY'S BOSTON BAKED BEANS
A candy recipe that originated in Boston, GA

2 cups raw peanuts, hulled   ½ cup water
1 cup granulated sugar

Preheat oven to 300 degrees.   Combine all three in a saucepan and cook until "sugary", about 10 minutes. Spread in a greased pan and bake for 20 minutes. Cool and break apart.

TRACEY'S ROCKY ROAD FUDGE

1 lb. Cocoa Candy Melts   1 cup chopped pecans
1 cup mini marshmallows

Melt coating "Melts" in top of a double boiler, stirring constantly. Add marshmallows and pecans. Line a 9x13 inch pan with foil and pour candy into it. Let it sit at room temperature till hard. Remove from pan, peel off foil and break into pieces.

NOTE: The microwave is the fastest way to melt Candy Melts. Use the defrost setting or 50% power. Place in glass bowl or 4-cup measuring cup. Microwave for 1 minute & stir. Microwave for another minute & stir. Continue at 30 second intervals, stirring after each until completely melted and smooth.

Manhattan is ready for Santa

70

AUNT CLARA'S TINY HOLLY WREATHS

30 large marshmallows
½ cup butter
1 tsp. vanilla
1 Tbsp. green food color

3½ cups corn flakes
Red Hots (candy)

Combine marshmallows and butter in top of double boiler. Melt completely over hot water, stirring frequently. Stir in vanilla and food coloring. Gradually and carefully stir in cereal. Drop by teaspoonfuls onto waxed paper, and shape, with hands, into tiny wreaths, about 2 inches in diameter. Decorate with tiny red hots while still warm so they will stick. Cool and store in airtight container. Makes about 33, 2 inch wreaths.

TURTLES

25 Caramels
2 Tbsp. heavy cream

1¼ cups pecan halves
4 1-oz. squares semi-sweet
    chocolate

Melt caramels with *heavy* cream in top of double boiler. Let cool 10 minutes. Arrange pecan halves in groups of 3 on lightly greased baking sheet. (1 for head & 2 for legs). Spoon melted caramel on top of nuts, leaving tips showing. Let set up about 30 minutes. Melt chocolate, stirring until smooth. Cool; spread over caramel top "turtles", do not cover tips. Makes about 24

Granny Says:
The older you get, the tougher it is to lose weight because by then your body and fat are really good friends!

71

Aunt Maggie's Potato Candy

A great old fashioned "hand-me-down" Christmas recipe.

1   cup warm, unseasoned, mashed potatoes
½ tsp. salt
2   tsp. vanilla
2   1-lb. boxes powdered sugar
1   1-lb. pkg. chocolate coating
⅔ cup finely chopped salted peanuts or flaked
      coconut

Combine potatoes, salt and vanilla in a 4-qt. mixing bowl. Sift powdered sugar over potato mixture, stirring and adding about 1 cup at a time. Mixture will be liquidy when the first sugar is added, then gradually begins to thicken. Stir until the consistency of stiff dough. Knead well. Add more sugar, if needed. Cover with a damp cloth and chill until a piece pinched into a ball holds it's shape. Shape all of the dough into ½ inch balls. Dip in melted chocolate, then roll in chopped peanuts or coconut. Makes about 92 small balls.

Sweetened Condensed Milk

Make your own....this works!

⅓ cup boiling water
¾ cup sugar
1   cup instant, nonfat dry milk powder
¼ cup butter
½ tsp. vanilla

Combine all of the ingredients in blender or food processor and process till thick and smooth. Refrigerate. This recipe makes 1¼ cups, the same amount in a 14 oz. can.

GRANNY'S BROWN SUGAR FUDGE
Also called "Penuche"

1 cup brown sugar, packed
1½ cups granulated sugar
⅓ cup light cream or half-and-half
⅓ cup milk
2 Tbsp. butter
1 tsp. vanilla
½ cup chopped pecans

Butter sides of a heavy 2-qt. saucepan. Combine both sugars, cream, milk and butter. Heat over medium heat, stirring constantly till sugars melt and mixture comes to rolling boil. If sugar crystals form on sides of pan, wipe them off. Cook to soft-ball stage (238 degrees), stirring only when necessary. Remove from heat. Cool to lukewarm, 110 degrees without stirring. Add vanilla and beat vigorously till fudge becomes thick and creamy. Quickly stir in nuts and immediately pour onto a buttered platter or shallow pan. Score in squares while still warm; cut when firm.
VARIATION: Use 2 ¼ cups (1-lb. box) of brown sugar instead of any granulated.

Biscuit and MoJo tell Santa they want *lots* of good doggie biscuits and toys for Christmas.

Mama & the Betsy Wetsy Doll

When I came into the Cooper family, I was only 5 years old. My mother had married my dad in California where he was in the Navy. He had come from a very large family in South Georgia consisting of 7 boys and 2 girls. Not only was I the first grandchild in the family, I was the *only* child in the family, with lots of doting aunts & uncles and the most wonderful Grandmother ever, whom everyone called "Mama". She and I became instant "buddies". I was her "shadow". She nick-named me "Flossie" and some of my uncles, who are now in their 90's, still call me Flossie.

Mama was quite a practical joker. But I'm getting ahead of my story.

It was my very first Christmas in Georgia and when we came from California in late 1937, I was as excited as any 5½ year old, as the whole family was preparing for Christmas. Aunt Judy, the baker and candy maker was preparing the most delicious cookies and scrumptious candies. Mama and I went out into her pine tree "forest" to find our Christmas tree. We chose a gorgeous 10 foot long needle pine that smelled heavenly. To this day I can smell a fresh pine tree and get all nostalgic inside.

Mama's house was designed, as were most of the houses in those days, with the bedrooms on one side of the house and the living room, dining room and kitchen on the other side. A long wide hall divided the two sides. Standing on the front porch, you could see all the way through the house to the well on the back porch! These were referred to as "shotgun" houses. All of the rooms had fireplaces (the only heat) so the doors were kept closed at all times.

The fragrance of that fresh pine tree in the closed-up living room and a fire going in the fireplace, created a fragrance that no Yankee Candle could ever duplicate.

I had asked Santa for a Betsy Wetsy doll. She was a rubber baby doll, with her own wardrobe trunk full of baby clothes, lots of little triangle shaped pink flannel diapers, tiny gold pins and a little baby bottle with a small hole in the nipple. There was a small hole in her mouth, so when you fed her, the water went right through her body and came out through the small hole in her fanny, wetting her diaper.

"Cool", as my grandchildren today would say!

I had been put to bed in one of the bedrooms across the hall from the living room where the adults were gathered around the fireplace in Mama's room, waiting for the out-of-town aunts & uncles to arrive. I kept getting out of bed and going into the living room to see if Santa had come. It was back from one of those trips that I fell asleep. When I woke up, it was Christmas morning. I rushed into the living room and sure enough, Santa had brought my Betsy Wetsy doll!

All day long I played with, fed and changed the wet diapers on my new doll. Except, of course, for the few trips, in between, to go outside to the "outhouse".
I didn't know Mama had been hiding behind one of the bedroom doors, listening to me exclaim "Oh, you've wet your diaper again!". She watched as I would open the diaper & exchange it for a clean one. It was on one of those "trips" that she decided to play a little joke on me. She went to the kitchen, chewed up some parched peanuts, placed the peanut "mess" into the diaper, pined it back up and waited for me to return. I went through my usual routine of "Oh, you've wet your diaper again!". But *this* time when I opened the diaper I saw Mama's peanut "mess". I threw the diaper closed in shock and then heard Mama laughing from behind the door.

This became a family joke that Mama delighted in telling many many times throughout the years. She and I would laugh about it until she passed away in 1972.

UP ON THE HOUSE-TOP

B. R. HANBY

B. R. HANBY

1. Up on the house-top rein-deer pause, Out jumps good old San-ta Claus;
2. First comes the stock-ing of lit-tle Nell; Oh, dear San-ta, fill it well;
3. Next comes the stock-ing of lit-tle Will; Oh, just see what a glorious fill!

Down thro' the chim-ney with lots of toys, All for the lit-tle ones, Christmas joys.
Give her a dol-lie that laughs and crys One that will o-pen and shut her eyes.
Here is a ham-mer and lots of tacks, Al-so a ball and a whip that cracks.

Chorus

Ho, ho, ho! who would-n't go! Ho, ho, ho! who would-n't go!

Up on the house-top, click, click, click, Down thro' the chimney with good Saint Nick.

Visions of Sugarplum Cookies

©EvanCraft 2004

RECIPES:

Extras::

GRANNY'S COOKIE TIPS

1. Place cookie sheets on rack in center of oven.
2. Cookies burn easily, so use a timer or clock - don't rely on your memory. If you're like granny, your memory isn't too reliable!
3. Done or not?
   A. Bars or squares are done when sides shrink from pan or top springs back when touched.
   B. Crisp cookies are done when they are firm and lightly browned on the edges.
4. Remove cookies from baking sheet with a wide spatula. Pretty cookies must have a good figure, you know! Unless otherwise directed, remove cookies from cookie sheet right after taking from oven, and place on wire rack to cool. Never overlap, pile, stack or store _warm_ cookies.
5. Cookie dough will melt and spread on a hot baking sheet, so have a cool sheet prepared for the second batch.
6. Scrape cookie sheets clean and wipe with paper towel to reuse them. Do not wash cookie sheet between batches of the same baking..
7. Store only one kind of cookie in a cookie jar. When stored together, cookies mix flavors. And _never_ store soft and crisp cookies together.
8. Crisp cookies should be stored in a container with a loose-fitting lid. If cookies soften and become limp and tired, freshen them in a 300 degree oven (slow) for about 5 minutes before serving.
   Soft cookies,. bars and squares should be stored in a tightly covered container or right in the baking pan, covered with foil. If cookies begin to dry,

add a piece of bread or slice of apple to supply
the needed moisture.. .

9. When using oven-proof glass baking dish, lower
the baking temperature 25 degrees.

10. Most important! <u>Always</u> read a recipe completely
through before starting to bake anything <u>and</u> be
sure you understand it and that you have all of
the necessary utensils & ingredients.

11. A tip from my Mother: Put all of the ingredients
out on the counter before you start. Then as you
use each ingredient, put it away. If you have any
thing left over, you've left it out. It <u>may</u> be the
type of ingredient you can still add.

12. Use shiny cookie sheets. Dark ones absorb heat
readily and cookies may burn on the bottom.

13. Grease cookie sheets lightly. Too much grease (or
cooking spray) may cause cookie to spread too
much and burn on the bottom and sides. I use
"Bakers Joy" or "Pam with flour".

14. Use baking sheets with little or no sides. Pans with
deep sides prevent cookies from browning.

PREPARING COOKIES FOR TRAVELING

1. For a delightful gift on Christmas or any other occa-
sion, send a box of cookies. Choose cookies that are
delicious but hardy, so they can withstand the trip. Soft
cookies are generally the best travelers.

2. Use a strong cardboard box or metal container. Line
with waxed paper or foil and put a cushion of crumpled
up waxed paper on the bottom.

3. Pack snugly in rows, with the heavy cookies at the
bottom. Tuck popcorn, or crushed waxed paper in the

holes to prevent jiggling.

4. Cover each layer with a cushion of waxed paper or paper towels, and don't forget to put an especially fat layer on top.

5. Tape box shut with wide sealing tape and print address on box in case label gets lost in shipping. Actually UPS is the best recommended way.

6. Be sure and print name, address and "Fragile, Handle with Care" & "Perishable" on front of package.

My 2-story red gingerbread doll
house is always under our
Christmas Tree.

JAMMIES
"Thumb-print" Cookies

1½ cups butter (3 sticks)	3 large egg yolks
1 cup granulated sugar	1 tsp. vanilla
4 cups sifted flour	Jelly (your choice)

Preheat oven to 325 degrees. Cream butter and sugar. Add flour and egg yolks; then add the vanilla. This will make a heavy dough. Roll into one-inch balls, press an indention in the center of each with your finger or the end of a wooden spoon. (not all the way through) Fill each indention with ½ teaspoon jelly. Bake on greased cookie sheets for 15 minutes. Makes about 68 cookies

After cookies cool, frost with this icing:
- **1 stick softened butter**
- **1 tsp. almond extract**
- **2 cups sifted powdered sugar**
- **1 tsp. vanilla**
- **Few drops of heavy cream**

Beat all ingredients together until spreading consistency.

Natalie helps Grandma trim the tree.

82

Aunt Judy's Heavenly Bits

¾ cup butter
2 cups flour
6 Tbsp. powdered sugar
½ tsp. salt
1 tsp. vanilla
1 cup chopped pecans
2 Tbsp. ice water

Preheat oven to 350 degrees. Mix butter with flour until it looks like fine crumbs. Add sugar, salt, vanilla, pecans and water. Knead well and then form into small thin rolls. Bake on ungreased cookie sheets 10 to 12 minutes, until golden brown. Roll in powdered sugar.
Makes 8 dozen.

Mexican Wedding Cookies

1 cup butter, softened
½ cup sifted powdered sugar
2 cups flour

2 tsp. vanilla
2 cups pecans,
    finely chopped

Preheat oven to 350 degrees. Cream butter and sugar till fluffy. Blend in flour, vanilla and pecans. Roll in small balls (or rolls). Bake on ungreased cookie sheets for 7 to 10 minutes. Roll in powdered sugar while still *warm*. (so sugar will stick to cookie) Cool, then roll in powdered sugar again.   Makes 2 to 3 dozen

Decorating Tip:
Put a tall red candle in an old fashioned canning jar; hold in place in the middle while you fill the jar with fresh cranberries.

83

White Chocolate Macadamia Nut Cookies

2¼ cups flour
1 tsp. baking soda
½ tsp. salt
1 cup butter, slightly softened
¾ cup light brown sugar
¾ cup granulated sugar
1 tsp. vanilla
2 large eggs
1 12-oz. pkg. white chocolate chips
1 cup macadamia nuts, coarsely chopped

Preheat oven to 350 degrees. Sift the flour, baking soda and salt together. Set aside. Beat butter, both sugars, vanilla and eggs together. Don't beat till too soft or the cookies will spread too much. Blend in flour mixture. Stir the chocolate chips and nuts in by hand. Drop by teaspoonfuls 2 inch apart on ungreased cookie sheets. Bake for 10 to 12 minutes. Makes about 6 dozen

Santa's Whiskers

½ cup butter
¾ cup sugar
1 tsp. vanilla
3 Tbsp. milk
1½ cups flour

½ tsp. baking powder
½ tsp. salt
¾ cup chopped cranberries
Shredded coconut

Cream butter, sugar and vanilla; beat in milk. Sift flour, baking powder and salt together and mix into creamed mixture. Stir in fresh cranberries. Divide dough in half and lay each half on waxed paper. Form into rolls, 8 inches long. (dough will be soft) Roll in coconut. Wrap and chill. Slice thin. Bake on ungreased cookie sheets at 375 degrees for 12 to 15 minutes.

GRANNY'S COOKIE EXCHANGE
Also called "The 13th Dozen Cookie Exchange"

Granny's not really big on baking a whole lot of different kinds of Christmas cookies (now that's she's older), so she and her friends get together and hold a "Cookie Exchange Party". Besides, Granny loves *any* reason for a "get-together"!

Here's how it works:

Granny invites 11 friends to her party. Each person, including Granny, bakes 13 dozen of *one kind* of cookie. This is one dozen of each kind for everyone to take home and the extra dozen for sampling at the party. Granny & her friends usually bake *more* for the "sampling" part!

Granny invites them at least a week before the party so they'll have plenty of time to bake the cookies. She sets a "beginning and ending" time for the party since everyone is so busy this time of the year.

Here are her simple rules:

1. Bring copies of the recipe to go with the cookies.
2. Don't bring a recipe that has to be refrigerated after baking. Don't want any of Granny's friends spending Christmas in the hospital with food poisoning.
3. Bring a large container to take the cookie assortment home.

Granny will set her dining room table with her most festive holiday tablecloth and arrange the cookies as they arrive She will have plates, napkins and lots of good drinks like hot apple cider, coffee, hot chocolate, etc. to wash down all those cookies!

Sound like fun? This is one of Granny's favorite holiday "doings"!

COOKIE SUGGESTIONS:

Granny says to pick cookies from this section of her cookbook. There are a lot of yummy ones!

GRANNY'S OLD FASHIONED "ICEBOX" COOKIES

Grannies <u>invented</u> "slice & bake" cookies and didn't know it!

BASIC ICEBOX COOKIES

1 lb. sweet butter	6 cups all-purpose flour
2 cups sugar	1 Tbsp. vanilla
1 large egg	Pinch of salt

Preheat oven to 350 degrees. Cream butter and sugar, then add egg, flour, vanilla and salt. Divide in half and place each half on a large piece of waxed paper and form into a long roll. Refrigerate overnight, or at least 8 hours. Slice each roll into rounds about ⅓ inch thick and place slices 2 inches apart on greased cookie sheets. Bake for 12 to 15 minutes till nicely browned.

BUTTERSCOTCH ICEBOX COOKIES: Same as above except add **brown sugar** instead of granulated sugar.

CHOCOLATE ICEBOX COOKIES: Add **¾ cup unsweetened cocoa powder** plus and additional **2 Tbsp. granulated sugar** and **5 cups flour** instead of 6 cups flour.

PEANUT BUTTER ICEBOX COOKIES

½ cup butter	2 cups all-purpose flour
½ cup creamy peanut butter	½ tsp. baking soda
1 cup light brown sugar	½ tsp. vanilla
1 large egg	1 cup chopped nuts

Preheat oven to 350 degrees. Cream butter, peanut butter and sugar together; add egg. Sift flour and soda together; add to creamed mixture; add vanilla and nuts. Shape into roll as in recipe above; chill overnight. Slice and bake for 10 minutes. Great taste.

WALNUT ICEBOX COOKIES

1 cup butter
2 cups packed brown sugar
4 cups flour
1 tsp. baking soda
1 cup chopped walnuts (4 oz.)

Cream butter and brown sugar together, add flour and baking soda, mixing well. Stir in nuts. Form into a roll as directed in Basic Icebox Cookies and refrigerate over-night. Preheat oven to 350 degrees. Slice roll into thin slices. Keep turning the roll so you won't have a "flat" side. Bake on ungreased cookie sheets for 10 to 12 minutes.
VARIATION: After shaping cookie dough into a roll, press into additional finely chopped walnuts, pressing lightly to coat well. When sliced, the walnut coated slices will look nice.

CREAM CHEESE ICEBOX COOKIES

1 lb. sweet butter
1 8-oz. package cream cheese, softened
1 cup granulated sugar
2 cups powdered sugar
6 cups all-purpose flour
1 Tbsp. vanilla

Combine all ingredients, beating well. Shape into rolls, as with the other icebox cookie recipes. Refrigerate till firm; then slice and bake in 325 degree oven for about 15 minutes.   Makes about 60 cookies.
NOTE: These cookies can be shaped into small balls; placed on greased cookie sheet, flattened with fork tines and then baked at 325 degrees for about 15 minutes. Double or triple recipe for Granny's Cookie Exchange!

Miss Fanny's Brown Sugar Cookies

This recipe was sent to me by Nancy Barwick Crew, one of my best friends in high school. She reminded me that Miss Fanny Clark made a batch of these for us to eat on the school bus every time our basketball team played an out-of-town game.

½ cup shortening	½ tsp. baking soda
1 cup light brown sugar	¼ tsp. salt
1 large egg	½ tsp. vanilla
1½ cups flour	Nuts, if desired

Cream shortening and sugar. Add egg; beat well. Combine flour, baking soda, and salt; add to creamed mixture. Add vanilla and mix well. Mold dough into a roll. Wrap in waxed paper and chill in refrigerator. Slice into thin slices and bake on greased cookie sheet in a 350 degree oven for 10 to 12 minutes.

VARIATION: Add ¾ cup chopped pecans after vanilla.

Granny Cookie Tips:

1. When cutting slice & bake cookies, slice with dental floss and keep rotating the roll so you won't have a flat side.

2. Avoid over-mixing cookie dough. Over-mixing will result in a tough textured cookie.

3. Bake cookies only until they are done. Over-baking creates a dry cookie. Underbaking creates a "doughy" cookie. Use the time given as a *guide* for doneness. Cookies are done if they retain a slight imprint when pressed lightly with a finger.

4. When a cookie recipe calls for quick-cooking rolled oats, use quick-cooking or old fashioned regular but <u>not</u> the instant breakfast kind.

Cornflake Cookies

1 cup butter
1 cup packed brown sugar
1 cup granulated sugar
2 large eggs
1 tsp. vanilla
2 cups flour
1 tsp. baking soda
½ tsp. salt
½ tsp. baking powder
1 cup corn flakes
1 cup flaked coconut
1 cup quick-cooking rolled oats
1 cup chopped pecans

Preheat oven to 350 degrees. Cream butter; add sugars, eggs and vanilla, mixing well. Sift dry ingredients together and add to creamed mixture. Stir in corn flakes, coconut, oatmeal and pecans.. Roll into small balls and place 2 inches apart onto greased cookie sheet. Bake for 10 to 15 minutes. Makes about 6 dozen

Easy Peanut Blossoms

1   18-oz. roll Pillsbury Peanut Butter Cookies
     (in the dairy case at grocery store)
3   Tbsp. sugar
36 Hershey Milk Chocolate Kisses, unwrapped

Preheat oven to 375 degrees. Shape pieces of cookie dough into one-inch balls; roll in sugar and place 2 inches apart on ungreased cookie sheet. Bake for 10 to 12 minutes, till golden brown. Remove from oven and, while *still on the cookie sheet*, immediately place a chocolate Kiss on top of each cookie, pressing down firmly. Remove from cookie sheet and cool.   Makes 36 cookies

Peanut Blossoms

This "scratch" version was a Pillsbury Bake-Off Senior Winner in 1957. It has always been very popular.

1¾ cups sifted flour
1 tsp. baking soda
½ tsp. salt
½ cup shortening
½ cup peanut butter
½ cup sugar

½ cup brown sugar
1 large egg, unbeaten
1 tsp. vanilla
Granulated sugar
48 Milk Chocolate
    Kisses

Preheat oven to 375 degrees. Sift flour, measure, then sift with baking soda and salt. Set aside. Cream shortening with peanut butter and sugars till fluffy; . Blend in egg and vanilla. Add sifted dry ingredients. mixing well. Shape teaspoonfuls into balls. Roll in granulated sugar and place on greased baking sheets. Bake in preheated oven for 10 minutes. Remove from oven. Top each with a candy Kiss, pressing down firmly so cookie cracks around edge. Return to oven bake 2 to 5 minutes longer. Makes 48 cookies

Diana Dorrance's Cinnamon Cookies

Mrs. Dorrance said her mother always made these for her at Christmas.

1 lb. sweet butter, softened
1 lb. box powdered sugar
4 large eggs, beaten
7 cups all-purpose flour

1 Tbsp. baking powder
1 Tbsp. cinnamon
1 large egg, beaten

Cream butter, sugar and eggs. Combine flour, baking powder and cinnamon; add to creamed mixture. Chill in refrigerator at least one hour. Roll out and cut into rounds. Brush with a beaten egg. Bake 350 degrees for 10 to 12 minutes.

SNICKERDOODLES
A Christmas classic and our best selling
"Miss Dee's Kitchen" cookie mix.

½   cup butter flavored shortening
1½   cups sugar
2   large eggs
2¾   cups all-purpose flour
1   tsp. baking soda
¼   tsp. salt
2   tsp. cream of tartar
2   Tbsp. sugar
2   tsp. cinnamon

Preheat oven to 400 degrees. Cream shortening, sugar and eggs. Combine flour, baking soda, salt, cream of tartar and add to creamed mixture. Shape into one inch balls. Combine 2 tablespoons sugar and the cinnamon; roll cookie balls into sugar/cinnamon mixture. Place 2 inches apart on ungreased cookie sheet. Bake in preheated oven for 8 to 10 minutes. For "soft & chewy", check after 8 minutes, Carefully lift off pan with spatula onto wire cooling rack and let finish cooling till firm. Makes about 5 dozen.

LEMON CAKE MIX COOKIES
A favorite, that grandchildren like to make.

1   18.25-oz. package Duncan   1 large egg
     Hines Lemon Cake Mix   ½ cup powdered sugar
1½   cups Cool Whip

Preheat oven to 350 degrees. Combine cake mix, Cool Whip and egg, beating with a spoon until well mixed. Roll into small balls and drop into powdered sugar, coating well. Place on greased cookie sheet 2 inches apart and bake for 10 to 12 minutes. Makes about 5 to 6 dozen.

Sugar Crinkles

1 cup shortening
1½ cups sugar
2 large eggs
1 tsp. lemon extract
1 tsp. vanilla

2½ cups flour
2 tsp. baking powder
½ tsp. salt
Extra sugar

Preheat oven to 350 degrees. Cream shortening and sugar together till fluffy. Add eggs, lemon extract and vanilla. Stir flour, baking powder and salt together; add to creamed mixture, beating well. Chill dough.
Shape into 1 inch balls and roll in the extra sugar; place on ungreased cookie sheets. Do not flatten. Bake 8 to 9 minutes till light color. Cool on cookie sheet just slightly; then transfer to wire cooling rack. Makes about 6 dozen

Ginger Crinkles

¾ cup shortening
1 cup sugar
1 large egg
¼ cup molasses
2 cups flour

1½ tsp. baking soda
1 tsp. cinnamon
½ tsp. salt
½ tsp. ginger
¼ tsp. allspice

Preheat oven to 350 degrees. Cream shortening and sugar together; add egg and molasses. Sift dry ingredients and add all at once to creamed mixture. Shape into walnut-sized balls and roll in additional sugar. Place on ungreased cookie sheet. Do not flatten. Bake for 8 to 10 minutes or until tops crack. Transfer to cooling rack.
NOTE: This dough does not have to chill.

GINGERKIDS

This recipe holds the gingerbread kids shape well. It's not too spicy. Just right for people who don't like real strong, spicy gingerbread cookies. I sold this as a cookie mix to stores for about 6 years.

5 cups sifted flour	3 tsp. ground ginger
1 tsp. baking soda	1 cup shortening
1 tsp. salt	1 cup sugar
1 tsp. ground nutmeg	1 cup light molasses

Preheat oven to 375 degrees. Sift flour, baking soda, salt, nutmeg and ginger together. Melt shortening; add sugar and molasses, mixing well. Gradually stir in *4 cups* of the sifted flour mixture and then work in the *remaining flour mixture with hands*. Roll out on a lightly floured cloth about ¼ inch thick. Cut out shapes and place on ungreased cookie sheet. Bake for 13 to 15 minutes. Remove to wire cooling rack. Cool complete and frost or decorate, if desired. The number of cookies depends on size of cutters.

Granny's Tips:

1. You don't have to be limited to gingerbread men cookie cutters. Stars, angels, etc. look equally as cute.

2. You can also use these for tree decorations.
Just make a hole in the top of each cookie with a drinking straw before baking. After baking, while still warm, reinforce the hole with the straw again. When completely cool, write names on the cookies with frosting and tie with a pretty narrow ribbon to hang on tree.

©1995 Delafield Stamp Company

Gingerbread Men

½ cup shortening
½ cup sugar
1 egg yolk
½ cup molasses
½ tsp. baking soda
1 tsp. baking powder
1½ tsp. ground cinnamon

½ tsp. salt
1 tsp. ground ginger
½ tsp. ground nutmeg
½ tsp. ground cloves
2 cups flour, sifted

Preheat oven to 350 degrees. Cream shortening and sugar; add egg yolk and molasses blending well.
Add baking soda, baking powder, salt and spices. Slowly add sifted flour. Roll out about ¼ inch thick on lightly floured cloth and cut out with gingerbread men cookie cutters. Keep cutter clean so dough won't stick. You can dip the cutter in flour after each cut. Place on ungreased cookie sheet and bake 8 to 10 minutes.
Makes 2 to 3 dozen

GREETINGS FROM OUR HOUSE TO YOUR HOUSE–

Emery, Dianne, Tisha, Tim, & Tracey

Our Family Christmas Card, 1958
Tish, Tim and baby Tracey

Hello Dolly Bars
Also known as 7-Layer Bars and Magic Bars

½ cup butter
1 cup graham cracker crumbs
1 cup flaked coconut
1 6-oz. pkg. semi-sweet chocolate pieces
1 6-oz. pkg. butterscotch pieces
1 14-oz. can sweetened condensed milk
1 cup chopped pecans

Preheat oven to 325 degrees. Melt butter in a 9x13-inch baking dish. Layer the ingredients in ORDER given, lastly pressing pecans slightly down into milk. Bake for 25 to 30 minutes. While still warm cut into 24, 2x3" bars. VARIATION: Sprinkle 1 cup red & green M&M candies on top and press down before baking.

Turtle Cookies

CRUST:
2 cups flour   ½ cup butter, softened
1 cup light brown sugar

CARAMEL LAYER:
1 cup pecan halves   ⅔ cup butter
½ cup light brown sugar   1 cup chocolate chips

Preheat oven to 350 degrees. Combine crust ingredients mixing till fine crumbs. Pat into an ungreased 9x13-inch pan. Sprinkle pecan halves over unbaked crust. Combine brown sugar and butter in a saucepan and cook over medium heat until it boils, stirring constantly. Boil for 1 minute. Pour over pecans. Bake for 18 to 22 minutes. Remove from oven and immediately sprinkle chips over top, allow to melt slightly for 2 or 3 minutes. Swirl with a knife for marbled look. Cool. Makes 3 to 4 dozen bars.

Coconut Pecan Bars

CRUST:

½ cup butter
½ cup light brown sugar

1 cup flour
¼ cup flaked coconut

Preheat oven to 350 degrees. Mix crust ingredients together, like pie crust, until crumbly. Press into an ungreased 8-inch square baking pan. Bake for 20 minutes. *Do not turn oven off.*

FILLING:

2 large eggs
1 cup light brown sugar
1 cup chopped pecans
½ cup flaked coconut

2 Tbsp. all-purpose flour
1 tsp. vanilla
Pinch of salt

Beat eggs till frothy; add brown sugar. Combine the pecans, coconut and flour and add to egg mixture. Stir in vanilla and salt. Pour over baked crust and return to oven and bake for 20 minutes. Cool in pan on wire rack. Cut into 1x2 inch bars. Sift powdered sugar over top and remove from pan. Makes 24 bars

Granny's Bar Cookie Tips:

1. Bar cookies are the easiest cookies to bake. You skip the rolling and cutting and there's only *one* batch to take from the oven! Cut the bars whole still slightly warm or completely cooled, unless the recipe states otherwise.

2. Spread bar cookie dough *evenly* in pan so all the bars will have the same thickness and texture. If some areas of the pan are spread thinly, those bars will overbake. A toothpick that comes out clean when inserted in bar cookies will be an indication that they are done.

Grandma's Pinwheel Cookies

You're going to make the following <u>twice:</u>

½ cup butter, softened   **½ tsp. baking soda**
1 cup sugar   **2 cups flour**
1 large egg   **1 tsp. vanilla**

Cream butter and sugar; add egg. Dissolve baking soda in a little bit of hot water and add to mixture. Add flour and vanilla. Set this aside.
Repeat the above recipe except add 1½ ounces Bakers semi-sweet chocolate squares, melted. (1½ squares)
On waxed paper, roll out the top white dough.
On a separate piece of waxed paper, roll out the chocolate dough the same size. Turn upside down on top of the white dough and peel off waxed paper. Press white dough onto the chocolate dough. Roll dough up jelly-roll fashion tightly, into a log, starting with the long side. Wrap with plastic wrap and refrigerate over-night or at least 8 hours.   Preheat oven to 350 degrees. Slice dough into ¼-inch thick slices. Place on lightly greased baking sheets and bake 10 to 12 minutes.

Maggie's Easy Brownies

1 cup butter, melted   ½ cup Hershey cocoa powder
2 cups sugar   1 tsp. vanilla
2 large eggs   ½ cup chopped pecans
2 cups flour

Preheat oven to 350 degrees. With mixer on medium speed, beat butter and sugar just until mixed; add eggs, one at a time. On low speed, add flou and cocoa. Stir in vanilla and pecans. Spoon into greased 8-inch square baking pan. Bake for 15 to 20 minutes. Cool, cut into squares.

Fruitcake Cookies

½ cup butter
1 cup light brown sugar
4 large eggs
3½ cups all-purpose flour
1 tsp. baking soda
½ tsp. ground nutmeg
3 tsp. buttermilk

1½ lb. candied fruits,
    chopped
1½ lb. chopped pecans
1 1-lb. box dark or
    golden raisins

Preheat oven to 350 degrees. Cream butter and sugar; add eggs, one at a time. Combine *three* of the cups of flour, baking soda and nutmeg together; add to creamed mixture *alternately* with buttermilk. Mix the candied fruits, pecans and raisins with the remaining ½ cup of flour. Stir into cookie mixture. Drop by spoonfuls onto lightly greased cookie sheet. Bake for 20 minutes. Makes 7 dozen cookies

This was my mother-in-law, Kitty Evans' old home in downtown Tallahassee FL. on 119 W. Bloxham Street.

Before it was sold it to the State to make way for an expansion of the Capital Complex, my sister-in-law, Katie Evans Tryon, an artist, painted this picture of it.

CHOCOLATE SYRUP BROWNIES

½ cup butter, softened
1 cup sugar
4 large eggs
1 cup flour
1 16-oz. can Hershey's chocolate syrup
½ cup chopped nuts
1 tsp. vanilla

Preheat oven to 350 degrees. Cream butter and sugar; add eggs,. flour, chocolate syrup, nuts and vanilla, blending well. Spread evenly on a greased 15x10x1-inch jelly roll pan. Bake for 20 to 25 minutes.

FROSTING:

| 6 Tbsp. butter | 1½ cups sugar |
| 6 Tbsp. milk | ¾ cup chocolate chips |

Combine butter, milk and sugar in saucepan; boil rapidly for 30 seconds, stirring constantly. Remove from heat and add chocolate chips. Beat until smooth. Spread evenly on warm brownies. Cut into bars or squares.

VARIATION: Bake in a greased 9x13-inch baking dish for a sheet cake instead of brownies.
Frost with the above frosting recipe.

"Kibitz" was a family
Christmas present,
1983

99

PARK'S BAKERY BROWNIES

When Mr. & Mrs. Tom Park closed their bakery in downtown Thomasville, Georgia in 1974, I was in the catering business. I had tested so many brownie recipes but couldn't quite get that authentic "bakery" look or taste. So I called Mrs. Hettie Park and asked her if she would give me their bakery recipe. She so graciously said yes and gave it to me over the telephone. (I still have my original hen-scratching notes from that conversation!) She also shared their bakery recipe for coconut macaroons with me. When we opened our own bakery in 1983, we must have sold *thousands* of these delicious brownies. They are dense and chewy! I've never shared this recipe with anyone until now.
I have reduced the recipe for the home kitchen.

Mix together <u>slowly</u> in mixer but *do not cream:*
1 **lb. 4 oz. sugar** (about 2¾ cups)
3 **oz. unsweetened cocoa powder** (⅔ cup + 3 Tbsp.)
7 **oz. shortening** (1⅛ cups)
¼ **oz. salt** (1⅝ tsp.)
4 **oz. light corn syrup** (¼ cup)
⅛ **oz. vanilla** (¾ tsp.)

Add & mix but *do not beat:*
6 **oz. eggs** (¾ cup)   2 **oz. water** (¼ cup)

Add & mix but *do not cream:*
12 **oz. sifted cake flour** (3⅓ cups)
4 **oz. chopped nuts** (1 cup)

Spread evenly in a greased 13x18x1-inch bakery pan (found in kitchen shops, it is called a "half-pan"). Place pan in another pan. Bake in preheated 400 degree oven for about 25 minutes, until it rises and *just falls.*
Do not overbake or they will be dry. Cool completely.
Ice with the following Bakery Brownie Icing.

Bakery Brownie Icing

2 cups sifted powdered sugar
¼ cup sweet butter, cut in pieces
1 cup granulated sugar
1 cup semi-sweet chocolate chips
½ cup milk
¼ tsp. salt
1 tsp. vanilla
2 Tbsp. Amaretto or Kahlua liqueur (optional)

Put the powdered sugar in a mixing bowl to have ready. Combine butter, sugar, chocolate chips, milk and salt in a medium saucepan. Over medium heat, bring to a boil, stir constantly until chips melt and mixture is smooth and creamy. Simmer for *exactly* 3 minutes, stirring constantly. Pour hot mixture into powdered sugar; add vanilla and beat until creamy. Add liqueur. Pour over the baked brownies and smooth with a long metal spatula. Icing will be firm & smooth like fudge when set. When cool, cut into 2½ inch squares with a very sharp knife.. Makes 70 brownies.. Cut smaller for party trays.

Rachel's Snow Ice Cream

Use only freshly fallen clean snow...a real treat for small children! Can be kept covered in the freezer.

2 large eggs
½ cup sweetened condensed milk
¼ cup sugar
1 Tbsp. vanilla
Freshly fallen snow

Combine the first 4 ingredients together and beat well. Scoop up a big bowl of snow and combine with the egg mixture. Drizzle maple syrup on top, if desired.

Bourbon Balls
A 1970's classic

2½ cups finely crushed vanilla wafers (about 60)
1 cup powdered sugar
1 cup finely chopped pecans
¼ cup bourbon
2 Tbsp. cocoa powder
3 Tbsp. light corn syrup
Additional powdered sugar

Combine cookie crumbs, powdered sugar, pecans, bourbon, cocoa powder and corn syrup in a bowl. With hands, shape into 1 inch balls. using about a tablespoon for each; place on waxed paper. Roll each ball in the additional powdered sugar. Place in tightly covered container and let them "ripen" for at least 24 hours. Serve within 2 weeks. Makes 3½ dozen

Rum Balls
A little different recipe, akin to the recipe above.

1 cup finely crushed vanilla wafer crumbs
1 cup powdered sugar
1½ cups chopped pecans
2 Tbsp. cocoa powder
2 Tbsp. light corn syrup
¼ cup Myers light rum
Additional powdered sugar to coat

Combine all, mixing well with hands. Shape in small balls and roll in the additional powdered sugar. Place on waxed paper and let dry for several hours. Store in airtight container. Makes 4 to 6 dozen (depending on size)

RICH CHOCOLATE CHIP TOFFEE BROWNIES

Lucy Barnes shared this scrumptious brownie recipe with us. She also shared the photo of her grandson Eli's first Christmas!

2⅓ cups flour
⅔ cup light brown sugar, packed
¾ cup (1½ stick) butter or margarine
1 large egg, slightly beaten
1 12-oz. pkg. (2 cups) Hershey's chocolate chips, divided
1 cup nuts, coarsely chopped
1 14-oz can sweetened condensed milk
1 10-oz pkg. (1¾ cups) toffee bits, divided

Preheat oven to 350 degrees. Stir flour and brown sugar together in a large bowl; cut in butter with pastry cutter until mixture resembles coarse crumbs. Add egg and mix well; stir in 1½ cups of the chocolate chips and the 1 cup of nuts. *Reserve 1½ cups of this mixture* and press the remaining onto the bottom of a greased 9x13-inch baking pan. Bake for 10 minutes. Remove from oven, *do not turn oven off.* Pour sweetened condensed milk evenly over hot crust; top with 1½ cups of the toffee bits. Sprinkle the reserved mixture and remaining ½ cup of chocolate chips over the top. Bake 25 to 30 minutes or until golden brown. Sprinkle the remaining ¼ cup toffee bits on top. Cool brownies in pan, placed on a wire cooling rack. When completely cool, cut into 24 bars.

Eli's First Christmas!
2004

103

Marshmallow Brownies

¾ cup flour
¼ tsp baking powder
¼ tsp. salt
2 Tbls. unsweetened cocoa
¾ cup sugar
½ cup shortening

2 large eggs
1 tsp. vanilla
½ cup chopped nuts
16-oz. pkg. mini marsh-
 mallows

Preheat oven to 350 degrees. Combine flour, baking powder, salt, cocoa and sugar; blend in shortening, eggs, vanilla and nuts. Spread in greased 9x13-inch baking pan. Bake 20 minutes. Don't turn oven off.
Scatter marshmallows on top of brownies, do not allow marshmallows to touch edges of pan; return to oven and bake for 3 more minutes.

FROSTING:
While brownies are baking, combine the following in a saucepan:
½ cup light brown sugar
¼ cup water
2 squares unsweetened baking chocolate
Bring to a boil and boil for 3 minutes. Remove from heat and add:
 3 Tbsp. butter
 2 Tbsp. vanilla
 1½ cups sifted powdered sugar
Mix well; spread evenly over marshmallows.   Cool.
Cut into 16 squares

Don't forget the Teachers.
These brownies would be nice!

Meg's Sugar Cookies

Unlike most sugar cookie recipes, this dough does not have to chill before rolling out cookies.

⅔ cup shortening	2½ to 2¾ cups flour
1¼ cups sugar	½ tsp. salt
2 large eggs	2 tsp. baking powder
2 tsp. vanilla	

Preheat oven to 350 degrees. Cream shortening and sugar; add eggs and vanilla, beating well. Sift flour, salt and baking powder together; add to creamed mixture. Roll out on lightly floured surface and cut into desired shapes. Bake on ungreased cookie sheets for 10 minutes. Remove immediately or they will stick. For tiny mini-size cookies bake for 8 minutes.
VARIATION: For coconut cookies, stir in ⅓ cup flaked coconut after adding flour mixture..

.

Wilton's Sugar Cookies

1 cup butter	1 tsp. vanilla
1 cup sugar	2¾ cups flour
1 large egg	2 tsp. baking powder

Preheat oven to 400 degrees. Cream butter and sugar till fluffy. Beat in egg and vanilla. Blend flour and baking powder together and add to creamed mixture, one cup at a time. Dough will be very stiff. Do not chill. Roll out and cut with desired cookie cutters. Bake on ungreased cookie sheets on the top oven rack for 6½ minutes. Watch closely. Makes 5 dozen really good tasting cookies. Decorate or eat plain, they're just that good!

Granny's Tip: Put some hot spiced cider in crockpot to serve friends with these delicious cookies. (p. 39)

Mini Cheesecakes

Use miniature muffin pans and mini paper liners

Crust:
- ¾ **cup graham cracker crumbs**
- 1½ **Tbsp. sugar**
- ½ **tsp. ground cinnamon**
- 2 **Tbsp. soft butter or margarine**

Preheat oven to 350 degrees. Place miniature muffin paper liners in 2, 12-cup miniature muffin tins.
Mix crust ingredients together, stirring with a fork or mixing with fingers. Press one teaspoon into each paper lined mini cup. Set aside

Filling:
- 1 **8-oz. pkg. cream cheese, softened**
- ¼ **cup sugar**
- 1 **large egg**
- 1 **tsp. vanilla**
- 1 **21-oz. can Cherry Pie Filling**

Beat cream cheese with electric beaters until smooth and fluffy. Add sugar slowly, beating well. Add egg and vanilla. Fill cups ¾ full. Bake for 12 minutes. Cool completely, then chill. When ready to serve, spoon a little bit of the cherry pie filling on top of each one. Be sure to include one of the cherries. Makes 24
NOTE: If you fill the cups to the top, it makes 17.

VARIATION: Use the regular sized muffin cups and place one vanilla wafer, flat side down in each cup. Spoon filling ¾ full. Bake at 350 degrees for about 20 to 25 minutes till centers are done.
Makes 12 mini cheesecakes

VanZeli's Pfeffernuesse Cookies
A festive traditional German cookie.

1 cup sugar
1 cup shortening
2 large eggs
½ cup dark molasses
1 cup cold brewed coffee (1 tsp. instant in 1 cup water
        works well)
½ tsp. black pepper
¼ tsp. ground cloves
¼ tsp. salt
1 tsp. ground cinnamon
1 tsp. nutmeg
¼ tsp. anise oil or 1 Tbsp. anise extract
Flour, add until able to roll out
Powdered sugar

Preheat oven to 350 degrees. Cream together sugar
and shortening; add eggs, mixing well. Stir in molasses,
then cold coffee and anise oil (or extract). Combine all
spices and add to mixture. Add flour, a little at a time,
until dough is stiff enough to roll into a long hot dog
shape. Cut into small pieces and bake on ungreased
cookie sheets. Bake for about 10 minutes. Roll in powdered sugar while still warm. Cool and roll again in powdered sugar.   This recipe makes a lot of cookies!

Flavorings

Mace...has a nutmeg flavor.
Anise......... has a licorice flavor.
Cardamom... belongs to the ginger family
Coriander... has a flavor like lemon peel & sage.
Cumin...in the carrot family, it's an Italian & Mexican
favorite.

$\mathcal{M}$ELTING $\mathcal{M}$OMENTS
An old holiday favorite with many variations.

³⁄₄ **cup butter (1½ sticks)**   ½ **cup powdered sugar**
1 **tsp. vanilla**   ½ **cup cornstarch**
1 **cup flour**

Cream butter; add vanilla. Stir the flour, powdered
sugar and cornstarch together and add to creamed
mixture. This dough will be very soft. Cover tightly and
chill in refrigerator for about 1 hour. Preheat oven to 375
degrees. Roll dough in 1 inch balls, which is a level teaspoonful. Place on ungreased cookie sheets 1½ inches
apart. Flatten lightly with a fork dipped in flour.
Bake for 10 to 12 minutes until just the edges are
brown. Remove while still warm and place on wire cooling
racks. Frost.

Frosting:
2 cups sifted powdered sugar
½ **cup soft butter**
**About 2 tsp. lemon juice, enough for spreading con-
     sistency**

Frosting variations:
#1 1 3-oz. cream cheese, softened
     1 cup sifted powdered sugar
     1 tsp. vanilla

#2 1 cup sifted powdered sugar
     2 tsp. melted butter
     1 tsp. vanilla
     Just enough milk to spreading consistency

#3 Tint ½ of the frosting with green food coloring
     Tint ½ of the frosting with red food coloring

HOLIDAY SPRITZ COOKIES

You need to buy a Spritz Cookie Press for these.
An added bonus: with a cookie press, you can also make
cheese straws, cream puffs, eclairs.

1	cup butter, room temperature	2	tsp. vanilla
2/3	cup sugar	2¼	cups flour
1	large egg	½	tsp. salt

Preheat oven to 400 degrees. In large mixer bowl, combine butter, sugar egg and vanilla. Beat at medium speed until light and fluffy. Reduce speed to low and add flour and salt till well combined. Fill cookie press, pressing onto ungreased cookie sheet in desired shapes... Decorate as desired. Bake for 8 to 10 minutes until set but not brown. Makes about 6 dozen.

VARIATION: Divide dough in half and tint with red and green food coloring, adding 3 or 4 drops to each half. NOTE: Wilton Enterprises sells a Spritz Cookie Press with 12 design discs. Their baking & cake decorating products can be found at Michael's craft stores.

THE TOP 10 FAVORITE CHRISTMAS COOKIES

Spritz
Thumbprints
Pecan Tassies
Bourbon Balls
Sugar Cookies
Cinnamon Stars
Gingerbread Men
Fruitcake Cookies
Melting Moments
Shortbread Cookies

O CHRISTMAS TREE

O TANNENBAUM

The Christmas tree has been celebrated in song and legend since the time of its first adoption as a Christmas symbol in the days of Luther. The stirring melody of this German carol is well known in America, and several states have adopted it for their official state song. An example is "Maryland, My Maryland."

Translated from the German
English version by Ruth Heller

GERMAN

Happily

1. O Christ-mas tree, O Christ-mas tree, O tree of green, un-chang-ing. Your boughs, so green in sum-mer time, Do brave the snow of win-ter-time. O Christ-mas tree, O Christ-mas tree, O tree of green, un-chang-ing.

2. O Christ-mas tree, O Christ-mas tree, You set my heart a-sing-ing. Like lit-tle stars, your can-dles bright Send to the world a won-drous light. O Christ-mas tree, O Christ-mas tree, You set my heart a-sing-ing.

3. O Christ-mas tree, O Christ-mas tree, You come from God, e-ter-nal. A sym-bol of the Lord of Love Whom God to man sent from a-bove. O Christ-mas tree, O Christ-mas tree, You come from God, e-ter-nal.

4. O Christ-mas tree, O Christ-mas tree, You speak of God, un-chang-ing. You tell us all to faith-ful be, And trust in God e-ter-nal-ly. O Christ-mas tree, O Christ-mas tree, You speak of God, un-chang-ing.

Desserts Yule Love!

CAKE TIPS

1. Pound Cakes are traditionally made with baking soda and not with baking powder. (There are exceptions) The volume is created by the beating of the eggs. That's why it's so important to add eggs one at a time, beating well after each addition. Don't grease the sides of the pan as the cakes, like angel food cakes, have to have something to cling to as it rises. Let cakes stand 5 minutes in pan before removing. Then, it helps to carefully run a table knife around the edge. Turn upside down on a wire cooling rack, place with another cooling rack and flip the cake over to it's top.

2. My mother once told me the most important step in making a cake is creaming the butter and sugar. She said that step could take as much as 10 minutes. Beating the room temperature butter till fluffy and *slowing* adding the sugar. You certainly don't want to beat it so much that you melt the butter, but you want it light and fluffy. Stop occasionally and scrape the sides and bottom of the bowl with your rubber spatula. This is true whether you beat with an electric mixer or hand creaming, like grandma used to do. And weren't her cakes *good!*

3. Whipped cream should double in volume and be fluffy and smooth. As much air as possible must be beaten into the cream. This is accomplished more successfully by hand-whipping with a wire whisk instead of an electric mixer. The cream must be as cold as possible. Chill the bowl. In summertime, when cream is often difficult to whip, pour the cream into the bowl, add the whisk, and put everything in the freezer for about 20 minutes. Beat cream only until a dollop dropped onto a plate will retain it's shape in a *soft* peak. <u>Be careful not to overbeat or you may end up with butter!</u>

To flavor whipped cream: just before serving, fold in 2 tablespoons per cup of fine granulated or powdered sugar.

4. Egg whites beat to greater volume if they are at room temperature. It is very important not to get a "speck" of yolk or grease in them which will keep them from thickening. The bowl in which they are beaten and the beaters must be thoroughly clean. Copper bowls are the preferred, but of course, most home kitchens do not have copper bowls. Otherwise use glass or stainless steel. Never use aluminum because that will discolor the egg whites, giving them a gray color.

5. Cream of tartar helps prevent from over beating. It stabilizes the egg white. Use 1/8 teaspoon per six egg whites or a dash per three egg whites.

6. When making a chocolate cake or brownies, instead of dusting the pans with flour after greasing, dust with dry cocoa so you won't have to deal with a white film on the outside of the baked layers.

7. Add a pinch of salt to the egg whites. Begin beating at a slow speed for about 1 minute or until egg whites are frothy. Gradually increase speed to medium and begin testing for stiffness as soon as they begin to mound up on the sides of the bowl.

8. When a recipe calls for "superfine" sugar, just process your regular granulated sugar a few pulses in the food processor till it's fine!

Baking With Liqueurs

Liqueurs are used in desserts such as cheesecakes, brownies, icings, glazes, etc. to add extra flavor.
Here are some of the more common ones often used.

Liqueur	Flavor
Kahlua	Coffee
Amaretto	Almond (made from apricot pits)
Chambord	Raspberry
Framboise	Raspberry
Praline	Pecan
Cointreau	Orange
Triple Sec	Orange
Grand Marnier	Orange
Curacao	Orange
Kirsch	Black Cherry
Irish Cream	Made from cream & Irish Whiskey
Creme de Menthe	Mint
Creme de Cacao	Cacao
Apple Brandy	Apple, ex: Applejack
Galliano	Made from herbs & spices
Southern Comfort	Made from bourbon, peach liqueur and fresh peaches

Dear Granny: How do you slice a cake layer in half evenly?

Answer: Insert toothpicks horizontally around the outside edge, marking the middle. Using a serrated knife, slice into the cake about 2 inches on one side, using the toothpicks as a guide.
Wrap a long piece of dental floss around the layer pulling it into the cut, tie floss once to hold the threads together. Then tighten the floss until it cuts all the way through making a nice clean, even cut dividing the layer in half.

1950'S Icebox Fruitcake

Almost like candy! I've been making this for 50 years.

1 16-oz. pkg. mini marshmallows
1 5-oz. can evaporated milk
1 14.4 oz. box graham crackers
1 6-oz. bottle red maraschino cherries, cut up
1 6-oz. bottle green maraschino cherries, cut up
1 7-oz. pkg. flaked coconut
1 qt. pecan halves

Melt marshmallows in evaporated milk in a saucepan, stirring constantly till smooth. Crush entire box of graham crackers.* In a very large bowl, mix cracker crumbs and melted marshmallows together. Add cherries, coconut and pecans. Mix thoroughly with hands and pat firmly in a well buttered 10 inch tube cake pan. Chill thoroughly. Turn out onto a cake plate. To serve, cut in *thin* slices because it's very rich. It will keep all through the holidays. Wrap tightly and refrigerate between servings. A sealed Tupperware cake keeper is good for this.

*NOTE: 1 box of graham squares = 4 cups of crumbs .
(if you want to, buy the box of graham cracker crumbs instead of crushing the whole ones)

Megan
&
Marissa
with Santa

ETHEL WEEK'S DEVIL'S FOOD CAKE
Truly old fashioned goodness!

First:
 ½ cup + 2 Tbsp. butter
 2½ cups sugar
 5 large eggs

Cream butter and sugar; add eggs, one at a time, beating well after each addition.

Next:
1 tsp. baking soda
1 Tbsp. cold water
1 cup buttermilk
4 squares Baker's unsweetened chocolate
2 cups sifted cake flour
2 tsp. vanilla

Preheat oven to 350 degrees. Dissolve baking soda in cold water; add buttermilk. Melt the chocolate over warm water and add after buttermilk, beating continuously. The mixture will be thick. Sift cake flour 3 times and add alternately with chocolate mixture to the butter/sugar mixture. Add vanilla. Pour into 3 greased and waxed paper lined 9-inch cake pans and bake for about 20 minutes, until toothpick comes out clean when inserted in center.
NOTE: You can melt chocolate in microwave for one minute, stirring halfway between.

OLD FASHIONED DIVINITY ICING:

1⅓ cups sugar	Pinch of salt
⅓ cup cold water	2 Tbsp. sugar
½ cup light corn syrup	1 tsp. vanilla
2 large egg whites	

Continued

Continued:
Put sugar, water and corn syrup in covered saucepan. Bring to a boil and keep covered till all the sugar crystals have washed down sides of pan by steam. Remove cover and boil until syrup spins a long thread (230 degrees) Combine egg whites, 2 tablespoons sugar and salt in a large mixing bowl and beat until stiff, but not dry, peaks form. Slowly pour the hot syrup into egg whites, beating constantly. Add vanilla and beat until spreading consistency.

NOTE: Ethel said to make this icing 2 times. The first time, stack the layers, icing in between each layer and then put a light coat of icing all over sides. This keeps the crumbs from spoiling the second layer of icing. Then make the icing again and completely ice the cake with a nice fluffy coating.

MOTHER'S SEVEN-MINUTE ICING:
An alternate icing to Ethel's Divinity Icing.

- 2 **large egg whites**
- ¼ **tsp. salt**
- 2 **tsp. light corn syrup**
- 1½ **cups sugar**
- ⅓ **cup water**
- 1 **tsp. vanilla**

Combine first 5 ingredients in top of double boiler. Beat one minute with electric mixer till well combined. Then cook, over simmering water, beating constantly for about 5 minutes. Add vanilla and beat one minute more.

Granny says: Remember: If a recipe says "sifted cake flour" it means to sift <u>before</u> measuring.
If it says "cake flour, sifted" it means to sift <u>after</u> measuring.

One-Egg Yellow Cake

In the 1930's this was called a "Dinette Cake",
It's ideal when you need a small cake.

1¾ cup cake flour, unsifted
¾ cup sugar
2 tsp. baking powder
¼ tsp. salt

⅔ cup milk
⅓ cup oil
1 large egg
2 tsp. vanilla

Preheat oven to 350 degrees. Sift flour, sugar, baking powder and salt together. Add milk, oil, egg and vanilla. With mixer on medium speed, beat until smooth, scraping the bowl occasionally. Pour in a greased and waxed paper lined 9-inch square baking pan.
NOTE: **BOSTON CREAM PIE:** While cake is baking, prepare a 3-oz. pkg. vanilla instant pudding mix and refrigerate. Cool cake layer, slice in half, hoizontally, to make 2 thin layers. Put pudding over the bottom layer. Place top layer on the pudding and frost the top of the cake only with chocolate icing. (page 151)

Earthquake Cake

1 cup chopped pecans
1 cup flaked coconut
1 (18.25-oz.) pkg. German
    chocolate cake mix
½ cup butter, softened

1 8-oz. pkg. cream
    cheese, softened
1 1-lb. box powdered
    sugar
1 tsp. vanilla

Preheat oven to 350 degrees. Combine pecans and coconut; spread over bottom of greased 9x13-inch baking dish. Prepare cake mix as directed on package and pour batter over pecans/coconut. In separate bowl, beat butter, cream cheese, powdered sugar and vanilla, mixing well. Drop by tablespoonfuls evenly over cake batter. DO NOT STIR. Bake for 45 to 50 minutes or just until cake tests done, do not overbake. Makes 15 servings.

Aunt Edna's Black Midnight Cake

If you like a deep, dark and delicious chocolate cake, this is it!

1 cup butter
2½ cups sugar
4 large eggs
1 cup unsweetened cocoa
   powder
2⅓ cups warm brewed
   coffee

3 cups sifted cake flour
1 tsp. salt
1 tsp. baking soda
2 tsp. baking powder

Preheat oven to 350 degrees. Cream butter and sugar together; add eggs, one at a time, beating well after each addition. Add cocoa. Sift flour, salt, baking soda and baking powder together and add to creamed mixture alternately with coffee. Pour into 3 greased and waxed paper lined 9-inch cake pans. Bake for 30 to 35 minutes, till toothpick inserted comes out clean. Turn out on wire cooling racks to cool, peeling off waxed paper. While cooling, prepare icing below.

VARIATION: If you'd like, you can make 2 layers and 12 cupcakes instead of 3 layers.

MARSHMALLOW SEVEN-MINUTE ICING:

1 cup sugar
¼ tsp. cream of tartar
2 tsp. cold water
1 Tbsp. light corn syrup

1 large egg white
8 large marshmallows
1 tsp. vanilla

Beat sugar, cream of tartar, water, corn syrup and egg white together with electric beaters; cook in top of double boiler for 4 minutes, beating constantly. Add marshmallows and continue beating for 3 minutes, or until soft peaks form. Remove from heat and add vanilla, beat 1 minute more.

Snowball Cake

2 pkg. (¼-oz. each) unflavored gelatin, dissolved in 4
       Tbsp. cold water
1 cup boiling water
1 cup sugar
⅛ tsp. salt
Juice of 1 lemon
1 20-oz. can crushed pineapple, *undrained*
1 12-oz. carton Cool Whip
1 large angel food cake, broken into 1 inch pieces
1⅓ cups (3½ ounce can) flaked coconut

Dissolve gelatin in cold water; add boiling water, stirring
to completely dissolve. Add sugar, salt, lemon juice and
undrained pineapple, stirring until sugar is dissolved.
Refrigerate until slightly thickened but not set. (consistency of egg whites) Fold in ½ of the Cool Whip.
Lightly grease the sides of a 3 quart round mixing bowl
and line it with waxed paper.
Beginning with pieces of cake, _alternate layers_ of cake,
and gelatin mixture. Let stand in refrigerator _at least_ 6
hours or until set.
Unmold on pretty cake dish. Frost with the remaining
Cool Whip and cover generously with coconut.
Refrigerate until serving time. Refrigerate between serv-
ings.   Makes 12 servings
OPTIONAL: Decorate with maraschino cherries.
This cake can easily be made the day before.

Over the river and through the wood,
to see little John and Ann;
We will kiss them all, and play snowball
and stay as long as we can.
                    Lydia Maria Child (1802-1880)

THE LORD & LADY OF CHRISTMAS CAKES

The main difference between a Lord and Lady Baltimore cake is: the Lord is a yellow cake, called a "gold cake"(using yolks of the eggs only) and the lady is a moist, 3 layer white cake, (using whites of the eggs only). They both have a fruit & nut filling and iced with a fluffy white cooked frosting.

LORD BALTIMORE CAKE

¾ cup shortening
1¼ cups sugar
8 large egg yolks,
   well beaten
2½ cups sifted cake flour

4 tsp. baking powder
½ tsp. salt
¾ cup milk
1 tsp. lemon extract

Preheat oven to 350 degrees. Cream shortening and sugar until light and fluffy. Add egg yolks; beat well. Sift cake flour and sift again with baking powder and salt. Add to creamed mixture *alternately* with milk, in thirds, beating well after each addition. Add lemon extract; pour into 2 greased and waxed paper lined 9-inch cake pans. Bake for about 20 to 25 minutes, until tested done. Turn out onto wire cooling racks and cool completely before icing.

Next: Make Mother's Seven-Minute Icing on page 119. Take out *2 cups* of the frosting and mix it with the combined fruits/nuts (below). Spread it between the 2 cake layers. Spread the *remaining* icing on top and sides of cake.

Fruit/Nut Filling:
1 cup mixed candied fruit, chopped
1 cup chopped toasted pecans
¼ cup blanched toasted almonds
½ cup macaroon cookie crumbs, toasted

Continued:

Continued:
Mix all of the above together, stirring into 2 cups of the icing, as stated above, spreading between and on top of the cake.

LADY BALTIMORE CAKE

6 large egg whites
⅛ tsp. salt
2 cups sugar, divided
3 cups sifted cake flour
3 tsp. baking powder

⅔ cup shortening
½ cup milk
½ cup water
1 tsp. vanilla
1 tsp. almond extract

Preheat oven to 350 degrees. Beat egg whites until frothy. Add salt; beat until stiff but not dry. Gradually beat in *one* cup of the sugar until very smooth and glossy. Sift cake flour, measure and sift again with baking powder. Cream shortening with remaining cup of sugar; add flour *alternately* with milk, water and flavorings, beating after each addition. *Fold* in egg white mixture. Pour into 3 greased and waxed paper lined 9-inch cake pans. Bake for 15 to 20 minutes. Cool in pans 10 minutes before removing to wire cooling racks.
Cool completely before icing.

FILLING:

1 cup sugar
¼ cup cornstarch
½ tsp. salt
1½ cups cold water
2 Tbsp. butter

2 Tbsp. grated lemon rind
½ cups chopped dates
½ cups chopped walnuts
½ cups chopped Maraschino
    cherries, drained

Combine sugar, cornstarch, salt, water, butter and lemon rind. Bring to a boil over medium heat, stirring constantly for one minute; cool. Stir in dates, walnuts and cherries. Place between the layers of cake.
Frost top and sides with Mother's Seven Minute Icing, page 119.

$175,000 CAKE

Every few years, a cake comes along, the origination is usually unknown, but it spreads like wild fire and becomes very popular. Such is the case with this $175,000 cake recipe. I found it on my "buddy", Google. It's very rich, more like brownies, than cake.

Bottom Layer:
1 (18.25-oz.) box German Chocolate Cake Mix
1 large egg
1 stick butter, slightly softened & cut into slices

Middle Layer:
1 12-oz. pkg. semi-sweet chocolate chips (2 cups)
1 cup chopped nuts (pecans or walnuts)

Top Layer:
1 8-oz. pkg. cream cheese, softened
2 large eggs
3½ cups powdered sugar (1 lb. box)

Preheat oven to 350 degrees. Grease and flour a 9x13-inch baking pan. (if glass dish, 325 degrees) Combine cake mix, egg and butter in mixing bowl and beat on *low* speed for a couple of minutes, *just* until crumbly. Press evenly into prepared pan. Sprinkle chocolate chips and nuts evenly over 1st layer. Beat softened cream cheese, eggs and powdered sugar together till creamy and carefully spread evenly over chocolate chips and nuts. Bake for 40 minutes. Don't overbake. Run a knife around sides to loosen before it cools. Cool 2 hours before cutting. Cut into 24 bars. *Keep tightly covered with Press'n Seal.*

Serving suggestions:

1. Serve with a scoop of vanilla ice cream.

2. Drizzle a little chocolate syrup on top of the ice cream and sprinkle a few chopped nuts on top.

3. Cut in one-inch squares. It would make a nice addition to a party tray

Never-Fail Angel Food Cake

1   cup sifted cake flour
1½ cups sifted powdered sugar
1½ cups large egg whites (about 12)
¼   tsp. salt
1½ tsp. cream of tartar
1   tsp. vanilla
½   tsp. almond extract
1   cup granulated sugar

Preheat oven to 375 degrees. Sift cake flour and resift with powdered sugar 3 or 4 times; set aside.

Place egg whites in mixing bowl and let stand at room temperature for 30 minutes. Then beat egg whites with electric mixer, gradually adding salt, cream of tartar and flavorings, beating till soft peaks form. Gradually add granulated sugar, 2 tablespoons at a time, beating until stiff peaks form. Sift the flour mixture over beaten egg whites and fold in gently, by one-fourths.

Pour into ungreased 10 inch tube pan. Using a table knife, gently cut through cake batter to remove any air pockets. Bake for 35 to 40 minutes.

Invert pan over wire cooling rack to cool cake completely. If tube pan does not have "feet", then invert over top of a soft drink bottle till cooled.

Granny's Angel Food Tips:

1. It's very important not to get one speck of yolk into the egg whites or they will not beat properly. First separate each one into a little bowl before transferring it into the beating bowl.

2. Separate the eggs while they are still cold, but always let the whites come to room temperature before beating.

3. To loosen the cake from side of pan, carefully run a long metal spatula between the pan and cake, being careful not to cut into the cake.

Cold Oven Fruitcake

1 cup butter
1 cup sugar
5 large eggs, beaten
1 lb. candied cherries
1 lb. candied pineapple
¾ cup cake flour

1 cup pecan halves
1 cup cake flour
½ tsp. baking powder
1 tsp. vanilla
½ tsp. lemon extract

Do *not* preheat oven. Cream butter and sugar till light and fluffy; add beaten eggs. Chop cherries and pineapple and put in large bowl. Add ¾ cup cake flour and coat fruit well. Add pecan halves. Combine the remaining cup of flour and baking powder; fold into creamed mixture; add coated fruits and flavorings. Pour into a greased 10 inch tube pan that has been lined on bottom with waxed paper. Place in a cold oven and turn oven on to 250 degrees. Bake for 3 hours. Makes 16 servings

Pecan Fruitcake
Also a cold oven cake

1 lb. butter
6 large eggs, beaten
2 cups sugar
3 cups flour
1 tsp. baking powder
2 tsp. vanilla

1 cup flour
½ lb. candied cherries
½ lb. candied pineapple
1 lb. pecans

Cream butter, eggs and sugar. Sift the 3 cups flour and baking powder together, add to creamed mixture; add vanilla. Chop candied fruits and nuts; toss with the one cup of flour, coating well. Add to batter. Pour in greased and floured 10-inch tube pan. Place in a cold oven and turn on to 300 degrees. Bake for 3 hours.
Makes 16 servings

Georgia Pecan Christmas Cake
For those who don't like candied fruit

1 lb. butter
2 cups sugar
6 large eggs
1 Tbsp. lemon juice
1 tsp. grated lemon peel
1 tsp. vanilla
¼ cup flour
1½ cups golden raisins
4 cups chopped pecans
3 cups sifted cake flour
1 tsp. baking powder
¼ tsp. salt

Preheat oven to 300 degrees. Cream butter and sugar till fluffy; beat in eggs, one at a time; add juice, peel and vanilla. Coat the raisins and nuts with the ¼ cup flour. Sift together the remaining 3 cups flour with the baking powder and salt. Gently fold in the fruit/nut mixture *alternately* with the creamed mixture. Spoon into greased and waxed paper lined 10 inch tube pan. Bake for about 1 hour and 50 minutes. Cool in pan. Remove from pan and add glaze below.

PECAN ORANGE GLAZE:
¼ cup sugar
¼ cup orange juice
¼ cup lemon juice
¾ cup chopped pecans

Combine juices and sugar in a small saucepan. Heat, but do not boil. Pour warm glaze over fruitcake, allowing to run down sides and center. Sprinkle chopped pecans evenly over top.

Little Pecan Rum Cakes

2¼ cups sifted cake flour	¾ cup milk
1½ cups sugar	1½ tsp. vanilla
3½ tsp. baking powder	4 large egg whites
1 tsp. salt	½ tsp. rum extract
½ cup butter, softened	¼ cup Myers light rum

Preheat oven to 350 degrees. Combine sifted flour, sugar, baking powder and salt in mixing bowl. Add softened butter, milk and vanilla; beat at low speed till well blended. Increase mixer speed to medium and beat for 2 minutes, scraping sides and bottom of bowl occasionally. Add unbeaten egg whites, rum extract and rum. Beat for 2 more minutes. Grease and waxed paper line a 9x13- inch baking pan. Grease the waxed paper. Bake for 35 to 40 minutes or until straw placed in center, comes out clean. Cool on cooling rack. Turn out on large cutting surface and cut into 1½ inch squares.

PECAN ICING:

½ cup butter	1 tsp. vanilla
3 cups sifted powdered sugar	3 cups very finely chopped pecans
Pinch of salt	
¼ cup rum	Rum for coating

With mixer, beat butter and sugar till fluffy; add salt, rum and vanilla. Beat till fluffy. Pour a teaspoon of the extra rum over little squares; spread icing all over and roll in chopped pecans.
Makes 40 little cakes, great for a party tray.

VARIATION: Instead of covering the entire cake squares with icing and rolling in pecans, just spread icing on top of each square and top with a maraschino cherry.

Tennessee Tipsy Cake

1-lb. box golden raisins
8-oz. box chopped dates or candied cherries, halved
2 cups Jack Daniel's Bourbon
Soak raisins and dates (or cherries) in the bourbon; cover and let sit overnight or 24 hours.

Next Day, First: drain fruits, reserving liquor. (hide it from Grandpa, you'll need it for the next step)

CAKE:

1½ cups butter, softened	5 cups sifted cake flour
2 cups granulated sugar	2 tsp. nutmeg
6 large eggs, separated	1 tsp. baking powder
1-lb. box light brown sugar	1-lb. pecans halves

Preheat oven to 275 degrees. Cream butter and granulated sugar till light and fluffy; add egg yolks, beating well. Add brown sugar and beat well to dissolve sugars.

Sift together 4½ cups of the cake flour with nutmeg and baking powder. Add flour mixture alternately with drained whiskey. Fold in soaked fruit.

Mix the other ½ cup flour with pecans and fold into batter. Beat egg whites till stiff but not dry; fold into batter, distributing evenly.

Spray a 10-inch tube cake pan with cooking spray. From a brown grocery bag, cut a circle to fit the bottom with a hole in the center and place in bottom of the pan. Spray paper with cooking spray. Pour batter in pan and bake for 3½ to 4 hours or until cake tester or straw comes out clean. Allow to cool in pan 15 minutes, before turning out. When almost cool, sponge sides and inside center with a bourbon-soaked cloth. Wrap the cake with this cloth and wrap with plastic wrap. Cover with foil and store in refrigerator to "ripen" for at least 3 weeks before serving. Slice thin. Makes 16 to 20 slices
NOTE: Also called Kentucky Bourbon Cake

Mother's Lane Cake

1 cup butter, softened
2 cups sugar
3¼ cups sifted cake flour
3 tsp. baking powder

1 cup milk
1 tsp. vanilla
8 large egg whites,
   lightly beaten

Preheat oven to 375 degrees. Cream butter and sugar until fluffy. Sift cake flour; then sift again with baking powder. Add flour and milk alternately to creamed mixture; add vanilla. Fold in beaten egg whites.
Pour into 3 greased and waxed paper lined 9-inch cake pans. Bake for 20 to 25 minutes.

FILLING:
8 large egg yolks
1 cup sugar
½ cup butter
1 cup chopped pecans
1 cup raisins
1⅓ cups grated frozen
   coconut (6-oz. pkg.),
   thawed
1 tsp. vanilla
½ cup bourbon

In top of double boiler, cook egg yolks, sugar and butter until mixture is thick, stirring constantly. Then add remaining ingredients. Spread hot mixture on layers. Stack layers.

One of my favorite pictures of my mother, Shirley Cooper 1938

Make ½ **recipe of a 7 minute icing** and frost sides and top of cake, page 119

131

Punch Bowl Cake

A North Carolina Christmas favorite. Put this cake in a very large glass bowl. A medium size glass punch bowl will work. You want the layers to show.

1 18.25-oz. pkg. yellow cake mix
2 3.4-oz. pkg. instant vanilla pudding mix
1 20-oz. can fruit cocktail, drained
2 8-oz. cans crushed pineapple, with juice
1 21-oz. can cherry pie filling
2 cups chopped pecans
2 7-oz. pkgs. flaked coconut
2 8-oz. containers Cool Whip
Maraschino cherries for garnish (optional)

Prepare cake mix according to package directions. Cool layers and break into 1 inch pieces.
Prepare one box of pudding mix as directed on package. Place pieces of 1 cake layer in bottom of large glass bowl. Spoon prepared pudding mix evenly over cake pieces; top with *half* of the fruit cocktail, 1 can of the pineapple, with juice, ½ of the cherry pie filling, 1 cup pecans and 1 package of the coconut. Spread 1 container of Cool Whip evenly over top.
Repeat the layers, ending with the other Cool Whip on top. Garnish with maraschino cherries.
Chill until ready to serve. Refrigerate any leftovers.
Makes about 36 servings

More Granny Cake Tips:

1. Fill cake pans about ⅔ full and tap on counter to get any air bubbles out.
2. Always cool a cake in the pan on a wire rack for about 5 minutes after removing from oven. Then remove from pan and finish cooling on a wire rack.
3. Don't frost a cake until it's completely cool.

Elegant Eclair Cake
A beautiful dessert

1 14.4-oz. box graham crackers

Make topping first so it can cool

TOPPING:

½ cup margarine	¼ cup milk
1 cup sugar	½ tsp. vanilla
½ cup cocoa	⅛ tsp. salt

Melt margarine; add sugar, cocoa and milk. Bring to a boil and cook one minute. Remove from heat; add vanilla and salt. Let cool.

Mix together:
2 3.4-oz. boxes Instant Vanilla Pudding & Pie Mix
3 cups milk
Fold in:
1 8-oz. container Cool Whip

<u>Putting it all together:</u>
In a 9x13-inch pan or pyrex dish, put a layer of <u>whole</u> graham cracker squares, covering the bottom of the dish. Spread ½ of the pudding mixture on crackers.
Put a <u>2nd layer</u> of crackers and top with the other half of the pudding mixture.
Then put a <u>3rd</u> layer of graham crackers and **pour the topping over the top.**
Refrigerate for 3 to 4 hours.

NOTE: It is better the next day.
When ready to serve, cut into about 15 squares, 3 across and 5 down and carefully lift out each square with a wide metal spatula. Top each square with a stemmed red maraschino cherry. It's very rich!

Japanese Fruit Cake

1 cup butter
2 cups sugar
4 large eggs
3 cups cake flour
1 tsp. baking powder
1 cup milk

1 tsp. vanilla
1 cup chopped pecans
1 tsp. cinnamon
1 tsp. allspice
½ tsp. cloves
1 cup raisins, cut up

Preheat oven to 350 degrees. Cream butter and sugar till fluffy. Add eggs, one at a time, beating well after each addition. Sift flour, resift with baking powder; add *alternately* with milk. Stir in vanilla. Divide batter in half. To *one* half, add pecans. To the *other* half, stir in spices and raisins. Each half yields 2 layers. Bake the 4 layers in 8 or 9-inch pans for 20 to 25 minutes or until wooden toothpick inserted in center comes out clean.

FILLING:

Juice & rind of 2 lemons
2 cups sugar
1 cup boiling water
1 8-oz. can crushed
   pineapple, undrained

3½ cups grated coconut
2 Tbsp. cornstarch
¼ cup cold water

Combine all ingredients except cornstarch and cold water. Bring to a boil. Dissolve cornstarch in cold water and add to pan; cook until thickens. Cool.
To assemble cake: alternating dark and light layers, spread filling between layers and on top.
Make the seven-minute icing on page 119 and frost the sides and top of cake. Makes 24 servings

Fact: When a recipe calls for 1 coconut:
1 medium size coconut, grated = 3½ cups
A 6-oz. pkg. of grated coconut can be found in the frozen section at grocery store. It equals 1⅓ cups.

Hummingbird Cake
A North Carolina prize-winning Christmas cake

3 cups sifted cake flour
2 cups sugar
1 tsp. salt
1 tsp. baking soda
1 tsp. cinnamon
3 large eggs, beaten

1½ cups salad oil
1½ tsp. vanilla
1   8-oz. can crushed
     pineapple, undrained
2 cups chopped bananas
1 cup chopped pecans

Preheat oven to 350 degrees. Combine dry ingredients in a large bowl. Add eggs and oil. Blend but <u>do not beat.</u> Stir in the remaining ingredients. Spoon batter into 3 greased and waxed paper lined 9-inch cake pans. Bake for 25 to 30 minutes or until cake tests done with a toothpick. Cool in pans for 10 minutes. Then turn out on wire cooling racks. Frost with the Cream Cheese Frosting below. Sprinkle top and sides with <u>additional </u>chopped pecans.

Cream Cheese Icing:
1 8-oz. pkg. cream cheese, softened
½ cup butter or margarine
1 tsp. vanilla
1 16-oz. pkg. powdered sugar, sifted

Beat all icing ingredients together until fluffy. Spread between layers, on sides and top of cake. Press chopped nuts generously into the frosting on the sides of the cake and sprinkle more nuts evenly on top.

Ask Granny

Dear Granny: What does it mean to "scald" milk?

Answer: To heat to just below the boiling point, when tiny bubbles appear around the edge of the saucepan.

White Chocolate Christmas Cake

½ cup butter
2 cups sugar
2½ cups sifted cake flour
1 tsp. baking powder
4 large eggs, beaten
1 6-oz. white chocolate bar, melted
1 tsp. vanilla
1 cup buttermilk
1 cup flaked coconut
1 cup chopped pecans

Preheat oven to 350 degrees. Cream butter and sugar till light and fluffy. Sift flour, resift with baking powder; add to creamed mixture with rest of the ingredients. Blend well and pour into 3 lightly greased and waxed paper lined 9-inch cake pans. Bake for 30 to 35 minutes till tested done with a toothpick.

WHITE CHOCOLATE ICING:
½ cup butter, melted
1 6-oz. white chocolate bar, cut up
6 Tbsp. buttermilk
1 lb. box sifted powdered sugar
1 tsp. vanilla

Combine butter, chocolate and buttermilk in a saucepan. Over low heat, stirring constantly until chocolate melts and mixture is smooth. Remove from heat; add sifted powdered sugar and vanilla, stirring until smooth. Frost cooled cake layers.
Garnish with chocolate curls or finely chopped pecans.

 Granny Says: "Don't be confused about "heavy cream" and "whipping cream", they are the same!"

CHERRY-PECAN POUND CAKE

1½ cups butter, softened
8 oz. pkg. cream cheese, softened
3 cups sugar
6 large eggs
3 cups sifted cake flour
Dash of salt
1½ tsp. vanilla
8 oz. jar maraschino cherries, well-drained, chopped
½ cup chopped pecans

Preheat oven to 325 degrees. Beat butter and cream cheese together with electric mixer for about 30 seconds. Slowly add sugar, beating until light and fluffy, about 10 minutes. Add eggs, one at a time, beating well after each addition. Turn mixer on low and add the cake flour and salt. Add vanilla. Gently fold in chopped cherries and pecans. Pour into a greased 10-inch tube pan and bake for 1 hour and 15 minutes or till cake tests done. Cool in pan for 10 minutes before turning out onto wire cooling rack. Cool completely.

AMARETTO GLAZE
1½ cups powdered sugar, sifted
2 Tbsp. milk or cream
1 tsp. vanilla or Amaretto

Beat together till smooth. Pour over cake and let run down sides. Decorate with additional cherries, cut in half and pecan halves, if desired.
Makes 16 servings

CARAMEL APPLE PECAN CAKE

2 cups self-rising flour
1½ cups sugar
½ cup shortening
1 cup milk

1 tsp. vanilla
4 large eggs
1 apple, finely chopped

Preheat oven to 350 degrees. Combine flour, sugar and shortening in mixing bowl. Add milk and vanilla and beat vigorously. Add eggs and beat for 2 minutes. Toss chopped apple lightly with a little flour and fold into batter. Pour into 2 greased and waxed paper lined 8-inch cake pans and bake for 30 to 35 minutes, or until tests done when toothpick inserted in center comes out clean.

CARAMEL ICING:
3 cups sugar, divided
1 cup butter
¾ cup whipping cream
1 tsp. vanilla
1 cup finely chopped pecans

Place ½ cup of the sugar in a skillet, stirring until dissolved and light brown. Combine remaining sugar, butter and cream in a saucepan. Bring to a boil. Add browned sugar and cook to the soft ball stage. Remove from heat and add vanilla and nuts. Spread between layers and on top of cake.

Granny's Tip:
Always buy cake pans with even-straight sides, not sloping sides. If they "nest" inside each other, they will make uneven layers. And choose shiny pans, not dark ones.

German Apple Cake

2 large eggs	1 tsp. vanilla
1 cup vegetable oil	1 tsp. baking soda
2 cups sugar	2 tsp. ground cinnamon
2 cups cake flour	1 cup chopped pecans
½ tsp. salt	4 cups chopped apples

Preheat oven to 350 degrees. Beat eggs and oil together till foamy. Add sugar, flour, salt vanilla, baking soda, cinnamon and mix well. Batter will be thick. Fold in chopped nuts and apples. Spoon into a well greased 9x13 inch baking pan and bake for 45 minutes.
NOTE: Chop the apples by hand, not in the food processor. I've done it both ways and the apples turn out better if chopped by hand.

CREAM CHEESE ICING:
2 3-oz. pkgs. cream cheese, softened
3 Tbsp. butter
1 tsp. vanilla
2 cups sifted powdered sugar

Beat cream cheese and butter together till creamy; add vanilla, mixing well. Add powdered sugar and beat till smooth. Frost top of cooled cake.

WARM CARAMEL SAUCE: *An optional cake topping*
½ cup butter
1 cup light brown sugar
¼ cup evaporated milk

Melt butter in a saucepan; add sugar and milk. Bring to a boil; boil for 2½ minutes. Drizzle over cake while cake is still warm.

SMALL APPLE CAKE

2 cups diced apples	1½ tsp. ground cinnamon
1 cup sugar	1 tsp. baking soda
1 large egg	¾ cup chopped nuts
1 cup cake flour	1 tsp. vanilla

Preheat oven to 375 degrees. Mix apples and sugar together. Let stand until sugar is dissolved. Add egg and beat well. Sift dry ingredients together and stir into apple mixture. Add nuts and vanilla. Pour into greased 8-inch square baking pan. Bake for 40 to 45 minutes. Just before cake is done make topping.

CARAMEL GLAZE #1:
½ cup packed brown sugar
½ cup granulated sugar
2 Tbsp. flour
1 cup water
½ cup butter
1 tsp. vanilla

Cook sugars, flour and water in a saucepan until clear. Add butter and vanilla; stir until butter melts. Pour over cake while both are still hot.

OPTIONAL::
CARAMEL GLAZE #2:

3 Tbsp. butter	3 Tbsp. whipping cream
3 Tbsp. packed brown sugar	½ tsp. vanilla
3 Tbsp. granulated sugar	

Bring all ingredients to a boil, stirring constantly. Boil for exactly one minute. Remove from heat and spoon over cake.

ᛒRANDIED ꝼRUIT ꞒAKE

This is a recipe given to me by my good friend, Agnes Gerock of Wilmington, NC. It's rather involved since it begins with a "starter" that takes several weeks to make. My problem was, Grandpa Emery wanted to eat the brandied fruit before I could get it on the cakes!

MOTHER STARTER:
1 cup sugar
1 cup peach juice
1 cup pineapple juice

Combine the above in a <u>glass</u> jar and stir with a <u>wooden</u> spoon. Keep at room temperature for 2 weeks. Do not cover except with cheesecloth. <u>Stir daily with the wooden spoon</u>   This makes 1½ cups starter.

Then: Day 1:
In a gallon glass jar combine:
1½ **cups starter**
2½ **cups sugar**
 1 **16-oz. can sliced peaches, cut up, with syrup**
Mix and stir each day for 10 days. Keep at room temperature. It will start to foam.

Day 10:
Add to jar:
2½ **cups sugar**
 1 **16-oz. can pineapple chunks, with juice**
Mix and stir each day for 10 days.

Day 20:
Add:
2½ **cups sugar**
 2 **10-oz. jars maraschino cherries, drained & chopped**
Mix and stir each day for 10 days.

Day 30:

You're ready to bake cakes. This starter makes 3, 10 inch tube cakes. I'm giving you the recipe for 1 cake. If you want to make all 3 cakes at one time, multiply the recipe below times 3.

FIRST:

Drain fruit into a large bowl. Pour the drained juices into 3 jars. These are your new starters. One to keep and two to give away. Treat these new starters just as before, starting with the Day 1 procedure above.. This process should be started within 3 days of receiving the starter juice. Otherwise the juice can be frozen to place on hold until ready..

BAKING *ONE* CAKE:

Preheat oven to 300 degrees. Grease 10" tube cake pan.

1 18.25-oz. pkg. Duncan Hines Butter Cake Mix
1 3.5-oz. pkg. vanilla instant pudding mix
4 large eggs
$2/3$ cup oil
$1/3$ of the drained fruit ($1\frac{1}{2}$ cups)

Beat together with a spoon. Do *not* use electric mixer. Stir in:

1 cup chopped pecans
1 cup chopped walnuts
1 cup flaked coconut

Pour into greased tube cake pan and bake for $1\frac{1}{2}$ hours or till tested done. Ice cake while still hot

ICING:

1 8-oz. pkg. package cream cheese, softened
$1/2$ cup butter
1 lb. box powdered sugar, sifted
1 Tbsp. vanilla

Beat all of the above together until creamy. Spread on hot cake.

Apple Streusel Pound Cake

STREUSEL:

1 cup packed brown sugar
¼ cup cake flour
1 tsp. ground cinnamon
3 Tbsp. butter

1 cup chopped apples
1 cup chopped nuts,
   pecans or walnuts

Mix the sugar, cake flour and cinnamon together. Cut in the butter until it looks like crumbs. Stir in the apples and nuts. Set aside.

CAKE:

½ cup butter
½ cup sugar
3 large eggs
1 tsp. vanilla

2 cups cake flour
1 tsp. baking powder
1 tsp. baking soda
⅓ cup orange juice

Preheat oven to 350 degrees. Cream butter and sugar till light and fluffy. Add eggs, one at a time, beating well after each addition; add vanilla. Sift flour, resift with baking powder and baking soda; add alternately with orange juice to creamed mixture. Spoon ½ of the batter into greased tube pan; sprinkle with ½ of the streusel mixture. Spoon other ½ of the batter evenly over streusel. (save remaining streusel)
Bake for 15 minutes. Remove cake from oven and sprinkle top of cake with the reserved half of the streusel.
Bake about 35 minutes or till tests done with a toothpick. Cool completely on wire cooling rack.

APPLEJACK BRANDY GLAZE:

3 tsp. Applejack Brandy or orange juice
1 cup sifted powdered sugar

Beat together with a whisk or spoon till smooth and pour over top of cake and let run down sides.

German Chocolate Pound Cake

1 4-oz. pkg. German Sweet Chocolate
1 cup butter
2 cups sugar
4 large eggs
2 tsp. vanilla
2 tsp. butter flavoring
1 cup buttermilk
3 cups sifted cake flour
½ tsp. baking soda
1 tsp. salt

Preheat oven to 300 degrees. Partially melt chocolate
over hot water. Remove and stir rapidly till melted; cool.
Cream butter and sugar; add eggs, flavorings and buttermilk. Sift flour and resift with baking soda and salt.
Add to creamed mixture, mixing well. Blend in chocolate.
Pour into a well greased 10-inch tube cake pan and bake
for 1 hour and 15 minutes, testing with a toothpick for
doneness. Remove from pan while still hot and place on
wire rack to cool. When thoroughly cool, pour glaze,
below over top of cake.
To serve plain, without glaze, Top each slice with a scoop
of vanilla ice cream and shave German Chocolate on top.

GLAZE:
1 4-oz. pkg. German Sweet Chocolate
1 Tbsp. butter
¼ cup water
1 cup sifted powdered sugar
Dash of salt
1 tsp. vanilla

Melt chocolate and butter in water of low heat. Mix powdered sugar and salt together. Blend in chocolate and
vanilla. Pour over top of cake.

Harvey Wallbanger Cake

The ultimate Christmas party cake. Better make
several!

1 18.25-oz. pkg. yellow cake mix
1 3.5 oz. pkg. instant vanilla pudding mix
4 large eggs
½ cup vegetable oil
½ cup orange juice
½ cup Galliano liqueur
2 Tbsp. vodka

Preheat oven to 350 degrees. Combine cake mix and
pudding mix in a mixing bowl; add eggs, oil, orange juice,
liqueur and vodka. Beat on medium speed 4 minutes.
Pour into greased and floured 9-inch Bundt or 10-inch
tube cake pan. Bake for 50 to 60 minutes or until
tests done. Let cool in pan 10 minutes, remove and
place on wire cooling rack. Spoon the glaze on while the
cake is still warm.

ORANGE GLAZE:
1 cup sifted powdered sugar
1 Tbsp. orange juice
1 Tbsp. Galliano liqueur
1 Tbsp. vodka

Mix all together with a wire whisk till smooth and pour
over top of warm cake. Lightly spread with a spatula so
it runs down sides.

Granny Wisdom

We don't stop laughing because we grow old,
We grow old because we stop laughing!

Coconut Pound Cake

1 cup butter
2 cups sugar
5 large eggs
1 7-oz. pkg. flaked coconut
1 cup milk
2 cups cake flour
1½ tsp. baking powder
½ tsp. salt

1 tsp. coconut flavoring
1 tsp. butter flavoring

Preheat oven to 350 degrees. Cream butter and sugar together; add eggs, one at a time, beating well after each addition. Add coconut and milk. Sift flour, resift with baking powder and salt; add to creamed mixture. Add flavorings, mix well. Pour into well greased and floured tube pan or Bundt pan. Bake for 1 hour and 15 minutes. Test doneness with toothpick. Turn out on wire cooling rack and turn over on another wire rack so rounded side is up. Brush on topping while still warm.

COCONUT GLAZE:
1 cup sugar
½ cup water
1 tsp. coconut flavoring

Combine sugar and water in a saucepan. Bring to a boil. Remove from heat and add flavoring. Drizzle on warm cake with pastry brush.

David Thomas is all "spruced up" for Santa!

GERMAN CHOCOLATE CAKE
The original 1950's recipe

1 4-oz. pkg. German
    sweet chocolate
½ cup boiling water
2½ cups sifted cake flour
1 tsp. baking soda
½ tsp. salt

1 cup butter, softened
2 cups sugar
4 large eggs, separated
1 tsp. vanilla
1 cup buttermilk

Preheat oven to 350 degrees. Melt chocolate in boiling water; cool. Sift flour, measure, then sift again with baking soda and salt. Cream butter and sugar until light and fluffy; add egg yolks, one at a time, beating well after each addition. Blend in vanilla and melted chocolate. Add flour mixture *alternately* with the buttermilk, mixing just until incorporated. Beat egg whites until stiff peaks form; *fold* into batter. Pour into three, 8" or 9" cake layer pans that have been lightly greased and lined with waxed paper. Bake for 30 minutes or until a toothpick inserted in center comes out clean. Cool in pan 10 minutes, then turn out on wire racks to cool.

COCONUT-PECAN FROSTING:

1 cup evaporated milk
1 cup sugar
3 egg yolks, slightly beaten
½ cup butter

1 tsp. vanilla
1⅓ cups flaked coco-
    nut, (3½ oz. can)
1 cup chopped pecans

Combine milk, sugar, egg yolks, butter and vanilla in a saucepan. Cook over low heat, stirring constantly until it thickens, about 12 minutes. Remove from heat; add coconut & pecans. Cool until spreading consistency. Spread between layers and on top of cake. Do not frost the sides. Makes 2⅔ cups

CARAMEL POUND CAKE

1   cup butter
½ cup shortening
1   1-lb. box dark brown sugar
1   cup granulated sugar
5   large eggs
3   cups cake flour
½ tsp. baking powder
1   cup sweet milk
1   tsp. vanilla
1   tsp. butter flavoring
1   cup chopped pecans

Preheat oven to 325 degrees. Cream butter, shortening and both sugars. Add eggs, one at a time, beating well after each addition. Sift flour with baking powder; add *alternately* with milk. Add flavorings and pecans. Pour into greased and floured 10-inch tube pan. Bake for 1 hour and 15 to 20 minutes.

CARAMEL PECAN ICING:
1½ cups dark brown sugar
1½ cups granulated sugar
¾ cup evaporated milk
¾ cup butter
2   tsp. vanilla
½ to ¾ cup chopped pecans

Combine both sugars, milk and butter in large saucepan. Bring to a boil and boil for 3 minutes. (time this) Remove from heat and add vanilla; beat to spreading consistency. Spread evenly over warm cake and let run down sides. May need to thin a little with a few drops of milk, but the warm cake should let icing spread easily. Sprinkle additional chopped pecans on top.

Grandma's Holiday Jam Cake

2 cups sugar
1 cup butter
3 large eggs
1 cup buttermilk
1 cup jam, your choice
3 cups sifted cake flour

1 tsp. baking soda
1 cup chopped nuts
1 cup chopped dates
1 cup golden raisins
1 medium apple, grated

Preheat oven to 350 degrees. Cream sugar and butter; add eggs, mixing well. Combine buttermilk and jam. Sift flour and soda together. Add alternately with milk mixture to sugar mixture. Mix well after each addition. Add nuts and fruits; mixing well. Pour into 3 greased and floured 9-inch cake pans. Bake for 35 minutes. Cool on wire cooking racks.l

FRUIT FILLING:

2 cups sugar
2 Tbsp. flour
1½ cups milk
1 cup butter
1 cup chopped nuts

1 6-oz. pkg. grated frozen
      coconut, thawed
1 cup diced dates
1 cup golden raisins
1 medium apple, grated

Mix sugar and flour in saucepan; add milk and butter. Cook until mixture thickens, stirring occasionally. Remove from heat; stir in nuts, coconut, dates, raisins and apple. Cool spread between and on top of cake layers. Do not put on sides of cake.

NOTE: Be sure and thaw frozen coconut before you start the cake.

BASIC 1-2-3-4 CAKE

1 cup butter
2 cups sugar
4 large eggs
3 cups cake flour

½ tsp. salt
3 tsp. baking powder
1 cup milk
2 tsp. vanilla

Preheat oven to 350 degrees. Cream butter and sugar; add eggs, one at a time, beating well after each addition. Sift flour and resift with salt and baking powder; add alternately with milk. Add vanilla. Pour into 2 9-inch cake pans and bake for 25 to 30 minutes.

MAYONNAISE CAKE

2 cups cake flour
⅔ cup unsweetened cocoa
    powder
1¼ tsp. baking soda
¼ tsp. baking powder
1⅔ cups sugar

3 large eggs
1 tsp. vanilla
1 cup mayonnaise
1⅓ cups water

Preheat oven to 350 degrees. Sift flour, cocoa, baking soda and baking powder together. In mixer bowl beat sugar, eggs and vanilla together till light and fluffy. On low speed, blend in mayonnaise. Add flour mixture and water <u>alternately</u>, beginning and ending with flour. Pour into 2 greased and floured 9-inch baking pans.
Bake for 30 to 35 minutes. Cool in pans for 10 minutes before removing to cooling racks

NOTE: I like to use left-over brewed coffee instead of water for a mocha flavor.

Continued

Continued:
CHOCOLATE ICING: (for either cake)

2 cups sugar   4 Tbsp. cocoa powder
½ cup milk   2 tsp. vanilla
½ cup butter   ½ tsp. salt

Combine all ingredients in saucepan and bring to a boil. Boil for exactly 2 minutes; cool thoroughly. Beat for 1½ minutes and frost cake.

HEAVENLY HASH CAKE

4 large eggs   2 tsp. vanilla
2 cups sugar   2 cups chopped pecans
1 cup melted butter   18 large marshmallows,
1½ cups self-rising flour   halved
¼ cup unsweetened cocoa
   powder

Preheat oven to 350 degrees. Beat eggs slightly; add sugar and butter. Blend flour and cocoa together; stir into egg mixture. Add vanilla and pecans. Pour into greased and flour 9x13-inch pan and bake for 30 minutes. Remove from oven and cover with the marsh-mallows, placing cut side down on hot cake.

ICING:
¼ cup melted butter   1 tsp. vanilla
½ cup evaporated milk
¼ cup unsweetened cocoa powder
1 16-oz. box sifted powdered sugar

Combine butter, milk and cocoa in a saucepan. Bring to a boil. Remove from heat, stir in powdered sugar and vanilla, stirring until smooth. Pour over marshmallows. Cut into 12 squares and serve with vanilla ice cream.

PINEAPPLE UPSIDE-DOWN CAKE

Old fashioned goodness; always a hit at church dinner-
on-the-ground meals.

¼ cup butter
⅓ cup evaporated milk
½ cup light brown sugar
1 20-oz. can pineapple slices, drained, reserving ¼ cup
    of the juice
7 marachino cherries

CAKE:

2 large eggs, separated	¼ tsp. salt
1 cup granulated sugar	¼ cup milk
1 cup sifted flour	1 tsp. pineapple extract
1 tsp. baking powder	1 tsp. vanilla extract

Preheat oven to 325 degrees. Melt butter in 9-inch
heavy iron skillet. Add milk and brown sugar, stirring
until sugar is melted. Place pineapple slices evenly over
mixture. Set aside.

Beat egg yolks with electric beaters at medium speed
until thick and lemon-colored; gradually add sugar, beating well. Heat reserved ¼ cup pineapple juice and milk
together, just till warm and add to egg/sugar mixture.
Add flavorings.

Sift flour, baking powder and salt together and add to
egg/sugar mixture.

Beat egg whites with electric beaters until stiff but
not dry. Gently fold into batter.

Spread batter over pineapple. Bake for 35 to 40 minutes. Cool in skillet 5 minutes. Run a knife around edge
of cake and turn out onto serving plate and place cherries in center of pineapple slices.   6 to 12 servings

Miss Kitty's Coconut Cake

My mother-in-law, Kitty Clyde Evans, was the best cook and baker! She didn't drive, but she was always on-the go with her lady friends from church. She always paid them back at Christmastime with a gift of one of her famous coconut cakes.

CAKE:

1 cup butter	½ tsp. baking powder
3 cups sugar	½ tsp. salt
1 Tbsp. vanilla	2 cups buttermilk
4 cups sifted cake flour	6 large egg whites
1 tsp. baking soda	

Preheat oven to 350 degrees. Cream butter and sugar until light and fluffy. Add vanilla. Sift together the flour, baking soda, baking powder and salt. Add to creamed mixture *alternately* with the buttermilk. Beat the egg whites until stiff peaks form; carefully fold into batter. Pour into 3 greased and waxed paper lined 9-inch cake layer pans. Bake for 25 to 30 minutes. Cool in pans for 10 minutes. Remove from pans and place on wire rack to cool completely. Frost with the 7-Minute Icing:

Miss Kitty

7-MINUTE ICING:

2 large egg whites
1½ Tbsp. light corn syrup
1½ cups sugar
Pinch of salt
5 Tbsp. water
1 tsp. vanilla

Combine egg whites, corn syrup, sugar, salt and water in top of double boiler. Beat on medium speed for about ½ minute.

Continued:

Continued:

Place over simmering water, not letting pan touch water, and beat constantly on high speed until stiff peaks form, about 5 to 6 minutes. Remove from heat, add vanilla and beat 1 or 2 more minutes or until spreading consistency. Spread between layers, on sides and top. Generously pat coconut into icing all around sides and on top. Makes a beautiful 3-layer cake.

✪ptional: 6-LAYER COCONUT CAKE

Make Miss Kitty's cake layers and when cool, split each layer in half, making 6 layers. See Page 116 for directions on splitting into even layers.

FILLING:

½ cup sugar	¼ cup butter
2 Tbsp. cornstarch	2 Tbsp. grated orange
1 orange juice	peel
4 large eggs, lightly beaten	1 tsp. orange extract

Combine sugar and cornstarch in a saucepan. Gradually stir in orange juice with wire whisk till smooth. Bring to a boil; cook, stirring constantly, for about 2 minutes or until it thickens. Remove from heat. Temper the eggs by stirring about ½ cup of the hot mixture into the eggs and returning all of it back into the saucepan. Slowly bring back to a gentle boil, stirring constantly, and cook for 2 minutes. Remove from heat and add butter, orange peel and orange extract. Cover with plastic wrap and refrigerate.

𝓐SSEMBLY:

Place one layer on cake plate. Spread with about ⅓ cup of filling. Repeat with 4 more layers. Then place the final 6th layer on top. Cover the sides with the 7-minute icing, then cover the top with icing. Press flaked coconut *generously* all over the sides and top. Refrigerate between servings..

PIES

General Directions for Crumb Crusts:

1. Put the dry ingredients in a small bowl.
2. Melt the butter and pour over crumbs.
3. Mix together with a fork until all of the crumbs are moistened.
4. Press into bottom & sides of buttered pie pan.
5. Bake at 350 degrees for about 10 minutes; cool, before filling so the filling won't be soggy.
6. Crumb crusts may be chilled, without baking.

The following are different types of Crumb Crusts:

1. Graham Cracker Crust: 1½ cups crumbs, 3 Tbsp. sugar, ¼ teaspoon ground cinnamon & 3 Tbsp. melted butter.

2. Coconut Crust: 1 cup graham cracker crumbs, 1 cup flaked coconut, 3 Tbsp. sugar & 4 Tbsp. melted butter

3. Vanilla Wafer Crust: 1½ cups fine cookie crumbs and 6 Tbsp. melted butter.

4. Macadamia Nut/Coconut Crust: 1½ cup vanilla wafer crumbs, ⅓ cup dry-roasted macadamia nuts (2 oz.) finely chopped, ⅓ cup flaked coconut and ¼ cup melted butter.

5. Corn Flake Crust: 2 cups crushed corn flakes, 3 Tbsp. sugar and 4 Tbsp. melted butter.

6. Gingersnap Crust: Good for pumpkin cheesecake. 1½ cups cookie crumbs, 3 Tbsp. sugar and 4 Tbsp. melted butter. (about 30 cookies = 1⅔ cups crumbs)

PIE TIPS

1. Always use all-purpose or cake flour for pie crusts.

2. Use very cold or ice water when mixing your pie crust and add very slowly, one tablespoon at a time, unless instructed differently.

3. Pie crusts should be rolled to about ⅛-inch thickness and about 2 inches larger than the pie pan you're using. Fit it loosely but firmly into pan.

4. Use a pastry brush and brush a little milk on the top crust, then sprinkle lightly with a little granulated sugar for a pretty golden crunchy finish.

5. A beaten egg yolk mixed with a teaspoon of water brushed on top crust will result in a golden color and a shiny finish.

6. Cool baked pies on a wire rack so air can circulate underneath. This helps prevent a soggy bottom crust.

7. Cream or custard pies should always be chilled before serving to get nice clean cut slices. Always keep these leftover pies in the refrigerator.

8. If you're going to buy pie crust, I suggest you buy the Pillsbury All-Ready Pie Crusts found in the refrigerator section at the grocery store. These come 2 to the package, are easy to use and taste just like homemade. Just follow the easy directions on back of box.

9. To prick or not to prick? For a *pre-baked* crust that's going to be filled with a cooked custard, any pre-cooked or ice cream filling, prick all over the bottom and sides well before you bake it. This prevents shrinking.

For further insurance, line the crust, bottom and sides with heavy duty aluminum foil, shiny side down. Fill with dried beans, rice or metal pie weights, purchased from a kitchen shop. This is referred to as "blind baking".

If you are going to bake your filling in the crust, do not prick. Example: apple pie.

10. Always preheat the oven before putting your pie or cake in it. (unless otherwise instructed).

11. To test oven temperature: Put an oven thermometer in the oven, turn oven on and preheat for about 15 to 20 minutes. Then check the thermometer to see if it is the temperature you set. Ovens will sometime vary by 25 to 50 degrees and this could ruin your cake or pie.

12. If baking in a glass/Pyrex dish instead of metal, lower the temperature by 25 degrees. And always bake pies in the **lower** ⅓ of the oven for a nice brown bottom crust.

13. If the top crust gets too brown before the pie is done, cover the edges lightly with strips of foil. Or buy the convenient PIE CRUST SHIELD at a kitchen shop, to prevent over-browning.

14. Do not freeze a cream or custard pie that has a meringue topping.

15. Place a cookie sheet under a double crusted pie or any pie that might spill or bubble over.

16. Patch any cracks in the pastry by taking small scraps, moisten the bottom and "paste" them over the cracks.

PASTRY FOR ONE CRUST

1 cup flour
½ tsp. salt
¼ cup vegetable shortening

1 Tbsp. butter, very cold
3 Tbsp. cold water

Place flour, salt, shortening and butter in food processor and pulse until it resembles coarse crumbs. Add water all at once with processor running. Process no more than 20 to 30 seconds. Shape into a ball with hands and chill for 30 minutes. Roll out on lightly floured cloth and proceed as for any other pie crust.

NOTE: For cooked filling: Prick all over with fork and bake in preheated 450 degree oven for 9 to 12 minutes, watch after 10 minutes. Cool before filling. See tip #9

Super Pie Crusts

EGG PASTRY:

3 cups flour
1½ tsp. sugar
1 tsp. salt
1 cup Crisco shortening
1 Tbsp. apple cider vinegar

5 Tbsp. ice water
1 large egg, beaten

Blend flour, sugar and salt together. Cut in shortening with a pastry cutter or pulse, if using a food processor. Mix the vinegar, water and egg together and add all at once. Mix well with a fork or pulse, (food processor). Divide into 3 pieces, wrap in plastic wrap and mash each flat into about a 3 inch circle. Chill for about 20 minutes before rolling out.
Makes 3, 9-inch pie crusts.

Recipe for 5, 9-inch pie crusts:

4 cups flour
1 Tbsp. sugar
2 tsp. salt
1½ cups Crisco shortening
1 Tbsp. apple cider vinegar
½ cup ice water
1 large egg

Follow directions above. Divide into 5 parts, wrap and chill at least 15 minutes before rolling out.

Granny's Pie Tip:
Cut drinking straws (paper, not plastic) into short lengths and insert through slits in pie crusts to prevent juices from running over in the oven and permit steam to escape.

Cream Cheese Pastry

This pastry is good not only for delicious little dessert "Tassies", but also filled with a seafood, chicken or other savory-type filling, they're great for hors d' oeuvres.

½ **cup butter, softened**
1 **3-oz. pkg. cream cheese, softened**
1 **cup sifted flour**
⅛ **tsp. salt**

Bring butter and cream cheese to room temperature. Combine all of the ingredients and blend with a pastry blender, as with any pie crust. Chill for 1 hour.
Shape into 24 small balls and press into ungreased 1¾ inch mini muffin tins, covering the bottom and sides. This dough should make 24 miniature shells.
For 48 mini shells, just double the above recipe.

For filling shells win a cooked filling, prick each one all over with a fork before baking. Bake at 375 degrees for 10 to 15 minutes., Cool before filling.

NOTE: You can make a lot of these little shells, baked, unfilled and frozen. Then when ready to use, thaw, warm in a 350 degree oven for about 5 minutes. Then they're ready to fill with your favorite cooked filling.

NOTE: A wooden tool called a "tart tamper", found in kitchen shops, would be a good tool to add the your kitchen baking collection. It is shaped so that the small end fits into the mini muffin tins and the larger end fits into the regular size muffin tin. Just place the ball of dough into the muffin tin and press the tart tamper to shape the little pie shell, getting neatly into the corners. I also use this tool when making graham cracker crusts for pies and cheesecakes to get a nice firm bottom and clean edges.

FILLINGS FOR CREAM CHEESE PASTRY TASSIES

In the South, we call these little jewels, "tassies".

LEMON:

Combine in a double boiler:
Grated rind of 2 lemons
½ cup fresh lemon juice
2 cups sugar
Add:
½ cup melted butter
Add:
4 large eggs, well beaten
Cook until thick, about 15 minutes. Cool and add:
2 Tbsp. orange flavored liqueur. (Cointreau) Chill.
When ready to serve, fill *baked* shells and top with sweetened whipped cream. Sprinkle a little grated lemon peel on top.

LEMON-CHEESE:

3 large eggs
¾ cup sugar
1 8-oz. pkg. cream cheese, softened
½ cup lemon juice
2 tsp. lemon rind

Beat eggs with a fork till thick and fluffy. Place in top of a double boiler and continue beating while adding sugar, lemon juice and rind. Cook over hot water until smooth and thick. Cool. Gradually blend softened cream cheese into custard, stirring until smooth. Fill baked tassie shells and top with whipped cream. Sprinkle a little grated lemon peel on top.

Granny's Tip

To bring butter or cream cheese to room temperature, remove from fridge 25 minutes before using.

Mincemeat:

1 jar prepared mincemeat
¼ cup Brandy

Preheat oven to 375 degrees. Mix mincemeat and brandy together. Fill *unbaked* pastry shells and bake for 25 minutes. This filling makes 36 mini tartlets

Pecan Tassies:

Chopped pecans	1 cup light corn syrup
3 large eggs, lightly beaten	Dash of salt
¾ cup granulated sugar	1 tsp. vanilla

Preheat oven to 350 degrees. Place about ½ teaspoon chopped pecans in each pastry shell. combine eggs, sugar, corn syrup, salt and vanilla.. Spoon about 1 table-spoon of this mixture over pecans, filling about ¾ full. Try not to spill any of the filling as it will be hard to remove tarts after baking. Place muffin tins on cookie sheet. They're easier to handle and catches any spillage. Bake for about 25 minutes. Cool; remove from pans. You may need to carefully run a knife around the edge of each one to remove it.
This recipe makes about 36 tassies

Peanut Butter Tassies

1 large egg	½ tsp. vanilla
½ cup sugar	1 cup peanut butter chips,
½ tsp. lemon juice	chopped

Preheat oven to 350 degrees. Fill each tart shell ¾ full. Bake for 20 minutes. Makes 24 tartlets

Assorted tassies on a party tray make a great little dessert tray.

German Chocolate Pie

1   4-oz. pkg. German sweet chocolate
1/4   cup butter
1 2/3 cups evaporated milk
1 1/2 cups sugar
3   Tbsp. cornstarch
1/8   tsp. salt
2   large eggs
1   tsp. vanilla
1/2   cup pecans, chopped
1 1/3 cups (3 1/2-oz. can) flaked coconut
1   9-inch unbaked pie crust

Preheat oven to 375 degrees. Melt chocolate and butter over low heat** Stir until blended. Remove from heat and gradually blend in milk. Mix sugar, cornstarch and salt; beat in eggs and vanilla. Gradually blend in chocolate mixture. Pour into pie shell. Sprinkle pecans and coconut evenly over filling. Bake for 45 minutes or until top is puffed. Filling will be soft but will set while cooling. Cool at least 4 hours before serving. Top with whipped cream, if desired. 10 to 12 servings

** Or melt in microwave oven by breaking the chocolate into pieces and combine with butter. Microwave for about one minute to melt, *stirring half way through.*

SWEETENED WHIPPED CREAM
1 1/2 cups whipping cream
4 Tbsp. sugar
1 tsp. vanilla

Beat all three together on medium speed with electric mixer until soft peaks form.

NOTE: Try the Chocolate Cool Whip or French Vanilla Cool Whip in the dairy case at your grocery store.

Aunt Chris's Cranberry Crumb Pie

A wonderful 2 layer pie...cheesecake-type bottom..a layer of cranberries wrapped in brown sugar, all topped off with a crunchy walnut streusel.

1 8-oz. pkg. cream cheese, softened
1 14-oz. can sweetened condensed milk
¼ cup lemon juice
1 Tbsp. brown sugar
2 Tbsp. cornstarch
1 16 oz. can whole cranberry sauce (not jellied)
1 9-inch unbaked pie crust

Preheat oven to 425 degrees. Bake pie crust for about 5 minutes. Remove and set aside. Reduce oven temperature to 375 degrees. Beat softened cream cheese with electric mixer until smooth and fluffy; add lemon juice, stir till incorporated and pour into pie crust. Combine brown sugar and cornstarch; add cranberry sauce. Spoon evenly over cream cheese mixture.

Topping:
⅓ cup flour   ¾ cup chopped walnuts
2 Tbsp. brown sugar
¼ cup butter, chilled and cut into small pieces

Combine flour, brown sugar and cut in butter till crumbly. Add walnuts and sprinkle evenly over cranberry mixture. Bake for 45 minutes till bubbly and golden brown. Cool.

Over the river, and through the wood,
when Grandmother sees us come,
She will say, "O, dear, the children are here,
bring pie for everyone"

Lyndia Marie Child (1802-1880)

163

Pumpkin-Pecan Pie

PUMPKIN LAYER:
1 large egg, lightly beaten
1 cup canned solid pumpkin (not pie mix)
1/3 cup sugar
1 tsp. pumpkin pie spice
1 9-inch unbaked pie crust

Combine first four ingredients, beating well. Pour evenly into bottom of pie crust.

PECAN LAYER:
2 large eggs, lightly beaten
1/2 cup sugar
2/3 cup light corn syrup
3 Tbsp. butter, melted
1 tsp. vanilla
1 cup pecan halves

Preheat oven to 350 degrees.
Combine eggs, sugar, corn syrup, butter and vanilla.
Beat well with a large spoon. Stir in pecans. Carefully pour over pumpkin layer. Bake for about 50 minutes or until center tests done with a toothpick.
Serve with French Vanilla Cool Whip.

Granny Wisdom:

Friends are the best collectibles!

CARAMEL APPLE PIE

½ cup sugar
¼ cup flour
1½ tsp. lemon juice
¼ tsp. salt
2 tsp. ground cinnamon
2-lbs. cooking apples, peeled and sliced thin
1 9-inch unbaked pie crust

Preheat oven to 375 degrees. Combine first 5 ingredients together, mixing well. Layer the apples and sugar mixture beginning with a layer of apples on the bottom and ending with sugar mixture on top. Bake for 20 minutes.
While pie is baking, make the topping:

TOPPING:
1 6-oz. pkg. (1 cup) butterscotch chips
¼ cup butter
¾ cup flour

Melt chips and butter together for one minute in microwave oven, stirring half way through. Cool slightly and stir in flour. Be sure everything is smooth.
Do not turn oven off.
When pie comes out of oven, spread topping evenly over top. Return pie to oven and bake for 25 minutes more. Serve with vanilla ice cream.

Granny's Pie Tip:
Glass type pie plates are better for baking pies. They are more apt to result in a nice brown bottom crust. Always bake pies in the lower ⅓ of the oven and lower the temperature 25 degrees.

Dutch Apple Pie

6 cups cooking apples, peeled and sliced
1 9-inch unbaked pie crust
1 cup sugar
2 Tbsp. quick-cooking tapioca
½ tsp. ground cinnamon
1 large egg, beaten
1 cup half and half
1 tsp. vanilla
½ cup walnuts or pecans, chopped
1 Tbsp. butter, cut into pieces
½ cup sharp cheddar cheese, shredded

Preheat oven to 350 degrees. Place all of the apple slices neatly in layers in pie crust. Mix the sugar, tapioca and cinnamon together. Combine the egg, half-and-half and vanilla and add the sugar mixture, stirring well. Pour over the apples. Bake for 45 to 50 minutes. Remove from oven and while still hot sprinkle with the shredded cheese. Serve warm.

Granny's Apple Tips:

1. One pound apples = 2 large or 3 medium

2. For a 9-inch pie, use 2 lbs. of apples, which is about 4 large or 6 medium. Some recipes call for 8.

3. It's better to *layer* apples with their sugar/spice mixture in the pie crust instead of mixing them all together. Sugar extracts moisture from the apples, producing a soggy crust. Layering the apples, fuses them together allowing them to retain their shape better.

CHERRY CHEESE PIE

Always a hit on the dessert table no matter what other desserts are there! A large 10-inch pie.

3 8-oz. pkg. cream cheese, softened
1 cup sugar
3 tsp. lemon juice
1 tsp. vanilla
4 large eggs
1 10-inch graham cracker crust
1 (21-oz.) can Cherry Pie Filling

Preheat oven to 325 degrees. Combine softened cream cheese, sugar, lemon juice and vanilla. Beat with electric mixer till smooth and lumps are gone. Add eggs, one at a time. Pour into crust & bake for 45 minutes. Top with cherry pie filling, and serve with lots of Cool Whip.

NOTE: This larger 10-inch graham cracker crust is found in the grocery store along with the other crumb crusts.

JAPANESE FRUIT PIE

½ cup butter
1 cup sugar
1 Tbsp. cider vinegar
2 large eggs
½ cup dark or golden raisins
½ cup chopped pecans
½ cup flaked coconut
1 9-inch unbaked pie crust

Preheat oven to 300 degrees. Cream butter and sugar; add vinegar and eggs, mixing well. Stir in raisins, pecans and coconut by hand. Pour into pie crust and bake for 35 to 40 minutes.

White Chocolate & Macadamia Nut Pie

¾   cup butter
1¼ cups sugar
1   tsp. salt
5   large eggs
1   cup light corn syrup
¾   cup Bailey's Original Irish Cream
1¾ cups white chocolate pieces
2   cups macadamia nuts, chopped
1   9-inch unbaked pie crust

Preheat oven to 300 degrees. Cream butter and sugar together. Add salt and eggs, blending well. Stir in corn syrup and liqueur. Add chocolate pieces and nuts, mixing well. Pour into pie crust and bake for 1 hour and 30 minutes. Cool completely before serving.
GARNISH: Chopped macadamia nuts and shaved white chocolate.

Grasshopper Pie

2 cups Oreo cookie crumbs
⅓ cup butter, melted
¼ cup creme de menthe
2 Tbsp. creme de cacao
7-oz. jar marshmallow creme
2 cups heavy cream, whipped

Mix cookie crumbs and butter together. Set aside ½ cup of the crumbs for the top of the pie and press the remaining into the bottom and sides of a buttered 9 inch pie pan. Stir creme de menthe and creme de cacao into the marshmallow creme, mixing well. Fold whipped cream into the mixture and spoon into pie shell. Sprinkle with the reserved ½ cup cookie crumbs. Freeze until ready to serve.
GARNISH: Whipped cream and chocolate curls.

GRASSHOPPER PIE #2

1¼ cups chocolate wafer crumbs
½ cup butter, melted
20 large marshmallows
½ cup milk
1 cup heavy cream, whipped
3 Tbsp. creme de cacao
3 Tbsp. creme de menthe
Few drops green cake coloring

Combine cookie crumbs and butter; blend well and shape
into a 9-inch pie pan. Chill. Melt marshmallows in milk
in top of double boiler, stirring until smooth. Cool thoroughly. Combine whipped cream, creme de cocoa, creme
de menthe and cake coloring and fold into cooled marshmallow mixture. Pour into chilled cookie crust. Chill until
firm. May be made a day ahead.
GARNISH: When ready to serve, grate chocolate on top
of pie and top each slice with a stemmed maraschino
cherry.

FRENCH COCONUT PIE

⅔ cup packed dark brown sugar
⅓ cup granulated sugar
2 large eggs
⅓ cup evaporated milk or heavy cream
1 tsp. vanilla
1⅓ cups flaked coconut (3½ oz. can)
1 9-inch unbaked pie crust

Preheat oven to 300 degrees. Combine first 6 ingredients, mixing well. Pour into pie crust and bake for 1 hour
or till pie tests done in center.

CRANBERRY-APPLE CHRISTMAS PIE

1 cup sugar
3/4 Tbsp. quick cooking tapioca
1/2 cup water
2 tart apples (2 to 2 1/2 cups) peeled & chopped
4 cups fresh cranberries, washed
1 Tbsp. lemon juice
Pastry for 2 pie crusts

Preheat oven to 450 degrees. Combine sugar and tapioca in a large saucepan. Add water and fruit. Bring to a boil; cook for 5 minutes. Remove from heat and add lemon juice; cool. Line a 9 inch pie pan with pastry. Pour in fruit and top with 2nd pastry; flute edges and cut slits on top crust. Brush some milk on crust and sprinkle lightly with granulated sugar. Bake for about 20 minutes

BUTTERMILK PIE
Right out of Granny's recipe box! A real winner!

1/2 cup butter, softened
2 cups sugar
3 Tbsp. flour
1/4 tsp. salt
1/2 tsp. nutmeg

3 large eggs, beaten
1 cup buttermilk
1 tsp. vanilla
1 9-inch unbaked pie
   shell

Preheat oven to 350 degrees. Cream butter and sugar. Add flour, salt, nutmeg and beaten eggs, beating well. On low speed, add buttermilk and vanilla, mixing well. Pour into pie shell and bake for about 45 minutes until center is set and nicely browned and toothpick comes out almost clean. 6 to 8 servings
NOTE: Remember to bake pies in the lower 1/3 of the oven.

Miss Charlotte's Turtle Pie

CRUST:
23 Nabisco chocolate wafer cookies, crushed
¼ cup butter, softened

Preheat oven to 350 degrees. Combine cookie crumbs and butter in food processor. Press on bottom and sides of a buttered 9 inch pie plate. Bake for 7 or 8 minutes. Cool.

FILLING;
½ gallon "pralines 'n cream" ice cream, softened
1 cup Heath Bits & Brickle

Spoon *half* of the ice cream into pie crust. Sprinkle all of the candy bits over evenly over ice cream. Spoon remaining ice cream on top, pressing down to firm. Freeze till hard.

When ready to serve, to each serving:
   Spoon sweetened whipped cream on top. Drizzle hot fudge sauce over whipped cream and sprinkle with chopped pecans. Top it off with a stemmed maraschino cherry. How's that for presentation!

Over the river and through the wood
Now grandmother cap I spy!
Hurrah for fun!
Is the pudding done?
Hurrah for the pumpkin pie!
Lydia Maria Child (1802-1880)

PECAN-CHEESECAKE PIE
This recipe combines two favorite desserts.

1 9-inch unbaked pie crust

CHEESECAKE LAYER:
1 8-oz. pkg. cream cheese, softened
⅓ cup sugar

¼ tsp. salt
1 large egg
1 tsp. vanilla

Beat cream cheese until smooth; add sugar, salt, egg and vanilla and continue beating until smooth.
Pour into pie crust

PECAN PIE LAYER:
3 large eggs, lightly beaten
1 cup light corn syrup
¼ cup sugar

1 tsp. vanilla
1 cup chopped pecans

Preheat oven to 350 degrees. In a medium bowl, lightly beat eggs with a fork. Add corn syrup, sugar, vanilla and pecans. Carefully pour over cheesecake layer and bake for 35 to 45 minutes until top is firm. Cool completely then chill for several hours or overnight.

Dear Granny: What is an "egg wash" and why do I want to use it?

Granny: An "egg wash' makes your top pie crusts and pastries look pretty. It also produces a "glue for sprinkling sugar on top.

Before baking: (options)
1. Basic egg wash: beat 1 whole egg with 1 tablespoon water and brush it on your pastry.
2. For a darker richer look, use milk instead of water. It produces a pretty golden finish.
3. If you want a shiny finish without color, simply use the egg white only, mixed with water.

CHEESECAKES

ALL ABOUT CRUSTS:

Basically the crusts for cheesecakes are pretty much like crumb crusts for pies. You need a special pan called a "springform" pan, found in specialty kitchen shops and large discount stores like Wal-Mart and Target. These pans come in sizes 8-inch, 9-inch, 10-inch and 12-inch. Kitchen shops also have the 3-inch and 4-inch sizes for individual cheesecakes. Start out with a 9-inch pan because most recipes call for it. If you want to invest in a 2nd one, the 10-inch is a good one. Each recipe will specify the kind of crust you need, but experiment with different crusts. Graham cracker crusts will go with just about any type of filling. Chocolate cookie crust go nicely with a chocolate filling. Gingersnap cookie crust is nice for pumpkin cheesecake.

The best way to line a springform pan with crumbs is this: butter the pan really good on bottom and about 2 inches up around the sides, so the crumbs will stick to the pan. Turn the pan on it's side and place a few crumbs into the pan. Place a piece of waxed paper underneath to catch the excess. Pat the crumbs firmly on the sides. Keep turning and adding crumbs until sides are well coated. Turn pan upright and press crumbs firmly on bottom of pan. Use the bottom of a small measuring cup to press the crumbs down firmly. (so when you pour your filling in, the loose crumbs won't "float") OR you could buy a wooden tool for this at a kitchen shop called "tart tamper". Bake the crust at 350 degrees for 10 minutes. OR you can put the pan in the freezer for 30 minutes. It's then ready to fill.

When a cheesecake is done, about an inch in the center should be a little "jiggly" and soft. It will firm up as it cools and after it has been chilled. It needs to chill at least 12 hours before serving.

Over-baking causes it to crack and become dry. But if it does crack at the end of baking, remember you can cover it up with pie filling, whipping cream, etc.

CRUMB CRUSTS:

I suggest you purchase a box of graham cracker crumbs and Oreo cookie crumbs at the grocery store.
General directions for Crumb Crusts are on page 155

Graham Cracker Crusts:

#1: For a 9-inch springform pan:
1½ cups cracker crumbs, 4 Tbsp. sugar, ¼ tsp. ground cinnamon and 6 Tbsp. melted butter.
#2: For a 10-inch springform pan:
1¾ cups cracker crumbs, 4 Tbsp. sugar, ½ tsp. ground cinnamon and ½ cup melted butter.

Chocolate Wafer Crumb Crusts:

#1: For a 9-inch springform pan:
1½ cups cookie crumbs, ⅓ cup sugar and 6 Tbsp. melted butter. (about 25 wafers = 1½ cups)
#2: For a 10-inch springform pan:
2 cups cookie crumbs, 2 Tbsp. sugar and 5 Tbsp. melted butter.

Oreo Cookie Crumb Crusts:

1½ cups cookie crumbs and 6 Tbsp. melted butter.
(about 30 cookies = 1½ cups)

Vanilla Wafer Crumb Crusts:

1¼ cups wafer crumbs and 3 Tbsp. melter butter.
(about 30 cookies = 1¼ cups)

Gingersnap Crumb Crusts:

2 cups cookie crumbs, 3 Tbsp. sugar and 6 Tbsp. melted butter. (24 gingersnaps = 1⅓ cups)

ᗩMARETTO ᑕHEESECAKE

CRUST: 9-inch graham cracker crust. Put crumb crust on bottom of pan only. Bake at 350 degrees for 10 minutes.

FILLING:
- 2   8-oz. pkg. cream cheese, softened
- 1¼ cups sugar
- 3   Tbsp. cornstarch
- 1   16-oz container dairy sour cream
- 5   Tbsp. Amaretto liqueur
- 1   tsp. vanilla
- ½ tsp. almond extract
- ½ tsp. salt
- 4   large eggs

Preheat oven to 350 degrees. In a large mixing bowl, beat the cream cheese till smooth; add sugar and cornstarch, beating well. Add sour cream, Amaretto, vanilla, almond extract and salt. Mix until well blended. On low speed of mixer add eggs, one at a time, mixing well after each addition. Pour into prepared crust. Bake for 60 minutes. Cool well on wire rack, then refrigerate till well chilled, at least 4 hours.

GARNISH: Top each slice with whipped cream and a sprinkling of toasted almonds or a few Italian Amoretti cookies.

Dear Granny: How do I measure baking pans, across the top or across the bottom?

Answer: Always measure baking pans across the top, right side up, *inside* edge to *inside* edge. Some pans are smaller on the bottom and taper out on the top, giving two different measurements.

Good Basic Cheesecake

When you can't choose, this classic is always a good choice.

CRUST: 9-inch graham cracker crust . Put in freezer for about 15 minutes, while you make your filling.

FILLING:
3 8-oz. pkg. cream cheese, softened
1 cup sugar
3 tsp. lemon juice
1 tsp. vanilla
3 large eggs

Preheat oven to 325 degrees. Combine cream cheese, sugar, lemon juice and vanilla. Beat until smooth. Add eggs, one at a time, mixing just until combined. Pour in prepared crust and bake for 45 minutes. Cool completely, then chill before serving. It slices better cold. Good topped with cherry, strawberry or blueberry pie filling.
GARNISH: Whipped cream or French Vanilla Cool Whip.

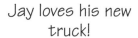
Jay loves his new truck!

Dianne's Cherry Cheesecake

CRUST:
1½ cups graham cracker crumbs
3 Tbsp. sugar
¼ tsp. cinnamon
4 Tbsp. melted butter

Combine crust ingredients and press in a well-buttered 9-inch springform pan. Bake 350 for 10 minutes.

FILLING:
3 8-oz. pkg. cream cheese, softened
2 tsp. lemon juice
¼ teaspoon salt
1 cup sugar
5 large eggs
1½ cups dairy sour cream
2 Tbsp. sugar
½ tsp. vanilla
1 21-oz. can Cherry Pie Filling, chilled

Preheat oven to 350 degrees. Beat softened cream cheese with electric beater till creamy, add lemon juice and beat till smooth. Add sugar, salt and eggs, all at one time. Beat at medium speed until well blended. Then beat for *10 minutes* more until mixture is smooth and lemon-colored. Pour into prepared pan and bake for 45 minutes. Remove from oven, leave oven on, and let cake stand for 20 minutes. With a spoon, stir sour cream, 2 Tbsp. sugar and vanilla together until sugar is dissolved. Spread on cake and return to oven for 10 more minutes. Cool. Chill. Spread chilled pie filling on top.

NOTE: When choosing Tapioca for thickening in puddings and fruit pies, choose Kraft Quick Cooking Minute Tapioca. It's a small 8-oz. red box.

Banana Split Cheesecake
A fun no-bake cheesecake

CRUST:
2½ cups graham cracker crumbs
½ tsp. cinnamon
¾ cup melted butter
Mix together and press into the bottom of a lightly buttered 9x13-inch glass dish.

FILLING:
2 8-oz pkg. cream cheese, softened
4 cups sifted powdered sugar
1 16-oz. can crushed pineapple, well drained
3 medium-size bananas, split and cut into fourths
1 12-oz. carton Cool Whip

Beat the softened cream cheese and powdered sugar together until smooth. Spread evenly over graham cracker crust. Carefully spread drained crushed pineapple over cream cheese. Then place the banana slices evenly over pineapple. Spread the Cool Whip evenly over pineapple and refrigerate for 6 hours. When ready to serve, garnish and cut into squares.
NOTE: If a 16-oz. can of crushed pineapple is not available, use 2, 8-oz. cans.

GARNISH:
chocolate syrup
maraschino cherries, with stem
chopped walnuts or pecans

Drizzle chocolate syrup and sprinkle chopped nuts over each serving. Top with cherry.

CHOCOLATE CHIP CHEESECAKE

CRUST: Chocolate Wafer Crumb Crust for 9 inch springform pan.

FILLING:
2 8-oz pkg. cream cheese, softened
1 cup sugar
4 large eggs
2 tsp. vanilla
1 cup miniature chocolate chips (6-oz. pkg.)

Combine cream cheese and sugar and beat until fluffy. Add eggs and vanilla all at once. Process in pulses until smooth. Fold in chocolate chips and pour into prepared crust. Bake 350 for 1 hour and 15 minutes or until center tests done. Cool thoroughly and then chill until thoroughly cold.
GARNISH: Put big spoonfuls of whipped cream all around edge of cheesecake and sprinkle with additional miniature chocolate chips.

Granny's Cheesecake Tip:

1. Always butter cheesecake pans well, otherwise the crumbs won't stick!

2. Always chill cheesecakes in fridge for at least 12 to 24 hours before serving. Otherwise they'll be soft and "mushy" and you won't get a nice clean cut.

3. Always refrigerate cheesecakes between servings, putting it back in it's springform pan.

4. If giving a cheesecake as a gift, put a cake circle in bottom of pan before preparing the crust.

Caramel Apple Cheesecake

CRUST: **Graham cracker crust** on bottom only of a well-buttered 9-inch springform pan. Bake at 350 degrees for 10 minutes. Cool.

FILLING:
2 8-oz. pkg. cream cheese, softened
½ cup sugar
2 large eggs
½ tsp. vanilla
4 cups apples, any variety, peeled and thinly sliced
⅓ cup sugar
½ tsp. cinnamon
1 12.25-oz. bottle caramel ice cream topping
1 cup chopped walnuts

Beat cream cheese and ½ cup sugar until smooth. On low speed add eggs, one at a time, beating well after each addition; add vanilla. Pour into prepared crust. Combine apples, ⅓ cup sugar, cinnamon and toss to coat apples. Spoon over cream cheese mixture. Bake at 350 degrees for 1 hour and 10 minutes. Chill for at least 8 hours. When ready to serve, warm caramel topping, stir in walnuts and pour over cheesecake, allowing to run down sides.

Granny's Cheesecake Tips:

1. Beat the cream cheese thoroughly, making sure all of the lumps are gone before adding other ingredients. Once the liquid is added, it's almost impossible to remove any lumps.

2. Use a timer to bake your cheesecake. It's too easy to get distracted and loose track of the time.

Frozen Mocha Toffee Dessert

Not a cheesecake, but a very elegant dessert that
I served many times at Horseshoe Plantation.

8 ladyfinger cookies, split
2 Tbsp. instant coffee crystals
1 Tbsp. boiling water
1 quart vanilla ice cream, softened
4 chocolate covered Heath toffee candy bars, frozen
    and then crushed (or pulsed in a food processor)
    to make 1 cup
½ cup whipping cream
2 Tbsp. white creme de cacao
1 additional toffee candy bar for garnish

Line the bottom an 8-inch springform pan with spit
ladyfingers, cut side up, cutting to fit. Line the sides,
2 inches up, with lady fingers cut in half, round side out.
(so when you unmold the dessert, the pretty round side
of the cookies will be showing)

Dissolve the coffee crystals in the one tablespoon of
boiling water; cool. Stir together the coffee, ice cream
and 4 crushed candy bars. Spoon into springform pan;
cover and freeze till firm. Just before serving, whip the
cream and creme de cacao, to soft peaks. Spread evenly over top of the frozen ice cream layer.
Garnish with additional broken toffee bar pieces.
Serves 8 to 10

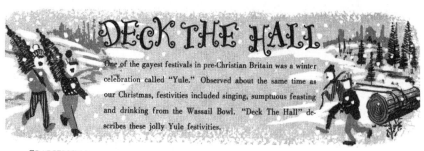

DECK THE HALL

One of the gayest festivals in pre-Christian Britain was a winter celebration called "Yule." Observed about the same time as our Christmas, festivities included singing, sumptuous feasting and drinking from the Wassail Bowl. "Deck The Hall" describes these jolly Yule festivities.

TRADITIONAL

WELSH

Rollicking

1. Deck the hall with boughs of hol - ly, Fa la la la la, la la la la.
2. See the blaz - ing Yule be - fore us, Fa la la la la, la la la la.
3. Fast a - way the old year pass - es, Fa la la la la, la la la la.

'Tis the sea - son to be jol - ly, Fa la la la la, la la la la.
Strike the harp and join the cho - rus, Fa la la la la, la la la la.
Hail the new, ye lads and lass - es, Fa la la la la, la la la la.

Don we now our gay ap - par - el, Fa la, la la, la la la,
Fol - low me in mer - ry meas - ure, Fa la, la la, la la la,
Sing we joy - ous all to - geth - er, Fa la, la la, la la la,

Troll the an - cient Yule-tide car - ol, Fa la la la la, la la la la.
While I tell of Yule-tide treas - ure, Fa la la la la, la la la la.
Heed - less of the wind and weath - er, Fa la la la la, la la la la.

Christmas Dinner at Granny's
Turkey, Soups, Sides & Salads

183

Butternut Squash Soup

I served this for guests at Gillionville Plantation in Albany, Georgia. With finger sandwiches, it made a wonderful hot lunch on a blustery winter day.

1 **butternut squash, peeled, seeded & diced (about 5 cups)**
2 **14-oz. cans chichen broth (4 cups)**
1 **Tbsp. tarragon**
1 **Tbsp. minced fresh parsley**
1 **medium yellow onion, chopped**
1 **clove fresh garlic, minced**
2 **Tbsp. butter**
2 **Tbsp. sherry**
¼ **cup flour**
Salt, black pepper & celery salt to taste
1 **cup half-and-half**

Bring squash, tarragon, parsley and chicken broth to a boil in large saucepan. Simmer on medium heat until tender. Saute onions and garlic in butter; add sherry and cook until soft. Add flour, stirring to mix well; add to squash mixture, stir and place in food processor. Pulse till smooth. Add salt & pepper, taste and then add celery salt to taste. Just before serving add half-and-half. Makes 6 servings

A nice accompaniment would be one of these:
1. Egg salad finger sandwiches, **4 hard-boiled eggs, peeled and chopped, ¼ cup chopped celery, 1 Tbsp. prepared mustard, 2 Tbsp. mayonnaise, salt & black pepper to taste.** Makes about 4 full sized sandwiches. Cut off crust & cut each sandwich into 3 "fingers"
2. Wedges of **Sweet Country Cornbread**, page 192
3. Warm buttered slices of **Zucchini Bread,** page 237
   Or Zucchini Bread muffins, same recipe.

CREAMY PUMPKIN SOUP
No frost on this pumpkin!

1   medium onion, chopped
1   celery rib, chopped
2   Tbsp. butter
1   16-oz. can solid packed pumpkin
2   14.5-oz cans chicken broth
1   tsp. salt
⅛ tsp. black pepper
¼ tsp. ground cinnamon
1

⅛ tsp. ginger
⅛ tsp. nutmeg
1   cup whipping
    cream

Saute onions & celery in butter for about 3 minutes until soft. Add pumpkin and *1 can* chicken broth. Bring to a boil, reduce heat, cover and simmer for about 20 minutes. Place in food process and process until smooth. Return to saucepan and add the *2nd* can of chicken broth, salt, pepper and spices. Simmer for 10 minutes, stirring occasionally. Stir in whipping cream, do not let boil. Garnish: sprinkling of nutmeg.   Serves 8

CREAM OF SPINACH SOUP
The guests at Horseshoe Plantation raved so about this soup that Mr. Dorrance (the Campbell Soup CEO!) took me aside and asked how I made it!

2   10-oz. pkg. frozen chopped spinach
⅓ cup chopped onions
2   14.5-oz cans chicken broth
4   Tbsp. butter
5   Tbsp. flour
2   pints half-and-half
½ to 1 tsp. tarragon
1   scant tsp. salt
⅛ tsp. white pepper

Continued

Continued:
Cook spinach with onions in chicken broth till just tender. (over-cooking will cause spinach to loose it's bright green color) Place in blender or food processor and process until smooth. Make a roux by melting the butter in small saucepan, over medium heat; add flour, stirring till smooth, Do not let it burn. Add this roux to the spinach, stirring constantly. Add half-and half and adjust seasonings.

Garnish: chopped boiled eggs, bacon bits, croutons or a thin slice of lemon   Serves 8

CREAM OF BROCCOLI SOUP

2 10-oz. pkg. frozen chopped broccoli
½ medium onion, chopped
3 cups chicken broth
4 Tbsp. butter
5 Tbsp. flour
Half-and-half
Salt & white pepper to taste

Cook broccoli and onion in chicken broth till tender. Place in food processor and pulse a few times, leaving small pieces of broccoli. Make a roux with butter and flour; add broccoli/onion/broth to roux, stirring constantly until thickened. Thin with half-and-half to desired consistency; add seasonings.

Garnish: croutons, sprig of parsley or sprinkle of paprika

Holiday Roasted Turkey

1. Rub the turkey lightly all over with olive oil and sprinkle lightly with salt outside and inside, if you're not going to stuff him. Place in a turkey roasting pan, resting on a roasting rack. If not using a roasting pan, place in a shallow baking pan, resting on a wire rack at least to raise him off the bottom of the pan. (I use a cookie cooling rack)

2. To stuff, lightly pack dressing into body cavities of turkey. Tie legs together with kitchen twine. Tuck wing tips over back and behind the neck. If stuffing the turkey, put enough stuffing in neck to fill it out nicely. Fasten neck skin to the back with skewers. Stuff cavity well, but don't pack tightly. Stuff the turkey *just before* roasting. Do not stuff ahead of time. If the stuffing is prepared in advance, it must be refrigerated.

3. Insert meat thermometer in the meaty part of thigh, and be sure it does not touch bone.

4. Cover the turkey lightly with aluminum foil. This is so it won't get brown too soon. Pour 2 cans chicken broth in bottom of pan. Believe it or not, this not only adds to the flavor of the turkey, but the moisture of the broth insures the tenderness of the meat.

5. Always place the turkey in a preheated oven, usually 325 degrees. Baste about every 30 minutes with pan drippings.

6. About 30 minutes before the end of roasting time, remove the foil to allow him to brown.

7. To test the doneness of the turkey, move the drumstick up and down. If the leg joint gives easily or breaks, the turkey is done. He is done when the thermometer registers 185 degrees and the juices run clear.

8. Let the turkey "rest" 15 minutes before you slice him. After all, he's been through quite an ordeal!

TURKEY ARITHMETIC

When buying a turkey, judge the size of the bird by thee number of servings you want. A good measure is ½ lb. per serving, not per person. Also, if you like leftover turkey and turkey sandwiches, take that in consideration when you choose the size of your turkey.

Here is an approximate table for number of servings.

Size of Turkey	# of servings
8 to 10 lbs.	16 to 20
10 to 14 lbs.	20 to 28
14 to 18 lbs.	28 to 36
18 to 20 lbs.	36 to 40
20 to 24 lbs.	40 to 50

TIMETABLE FOR ROASTING A TURKEY

Weight	Oven Temp.	Appx. cooking time
8 to 12 lbs.	325 degrees	4 to 4 /2 hrs.
12 to 16 lbs.	300 degrees	4 to 5 hrs.
16 to 20 lbs.	300 degrees	5 to 5½ hrs.
20 to 24 lbs.	300 degrees	5½ to 6 hrs.

Granny Says:

When preparing fresh broccoli, cut off and discard the tough ends of the stalks, leaving about 2 inches attached to the florets.
Cut the broccoli lengthwise into serving size slices and then with a potato peeler, peel the tough outer layer from the stalks.

EMERY'S OYSTER DRESSING

It probably makes little or no difference how oysters are added when making oyster dressing. Most people just stir them in but, the Virgo always comes out in Emery when he cooks.

1 recipe, Miss Dee's Corn Bread Dressing, 192
1 Pint, Fresh Standard Size Oysters

NOTE: When preparing the dressing, reserve one of those cans of chicken broth for the following step.

Preheat oven to 350 degrees. Drain the liquid from the oysters into the dressing mixture and stir thoroughly to blend in flavor. Then add as much of the second can of chicken broth as needed to bring dressing to the desired consistency. It should be very moist but, not soupy. Place half of the dressing mixture in a greased 9x13 inch baking dish. Layer the oysters evenly and then cover with the other half of the dressing mixture. Bake for approximately one hour, or until golden brown on top.

EMERY'S GIBLET GRAVY

Giblets and neck from turkey
1   small onion, chopped
2   stalks celery hearts, chopped
4   cups water
1   10½ oz can chicken broth
2   Tbsp. cornstarch dissolved in ¼ cup cold water
2   hard boiled eggs, chopped

Continued

Continued:

Combine giblets, neck, onion, celery and water in medium size sauce pan. Bring to a boil, reduce heat and simmer for 15 minutes. Remove liver and continue to simmer until meat is tender (about an hour and a half). Remove neck and giblets to chopping board and set boiler aside. After cooling to touch, strip the meat from the neck with your fingers, discard the bones and coarsely chop the neck meat, the liver and gizzard. Return this to the pot and add the can of chicken broth along with a little of the drippings from the turkey pan. (Reserve some of these drippings for your dressing) Bring this mixture back to a boil and gradually stir in the dissolved corn-starch, a little at the time, until the gravy assumes the desired thickness. Remove from heat, add the chopped eggs and proceed to *season to taste*. This the most important step. Remember, the chicken broth has salt so you may, or may not, want to add more. I use salt, (sea salt is best) Morton's Nature's Seasoning, black pepper and a little MSG. The MSG makes a wonderful difference but, if you are allergic to it, leave it out. As with all seasoning, it is best to add a little and taste until you get it just right.

Grandpa Emery takes a break!

Sweet Country Cornbread

1 cup self-rising flour
1 cup self-rising cornmeal
½ cup sugar
2 tsp. baking powder

2 large eggs
⅓ cup melted butter
1 cup milk

Preheat oven to 425 degrees. Spray a 9 or 10 inch black iron skillet with cooking spray and place in hot oven. This is the secret to a crusty cornbread bottom. Whisk the flour, cornmeal, sugar and baking powder together. In a separate bowl, combine eggs, butter and milk. Pour into the dry mixture and stir just until moistened. Pour in hot greased skillet and bake for 25 to 30 minutes until golden brown. Delicious eaten with a lot of sweet butter or crumbled for dressing.

Miss Dee's Cornbread Dressing

1 16-oz. pkg. Pepperidge Farm Cornbread Dressing Mix
½ cup chopped onions
½ cup chopped bell peppers
¼ cup chopped celery
2 Tbsp. butter
1 large raw egg
2 hard-boiled eggs, chopped
Drippings from turkey pan
2 10½ oz. cans chicken broth

Preheat oven to 350 degrees. Saute onions, bell pepper and celery in butter. Then mix everything together, using the drippings and as much chicken broth as needed to make very moist but not soupy. Pour into a greased 9x13-inch baking dish and bake for 1 hour.
Makes 8-10 servings

Sweet Potato-Apple Casserole

4 large cooking apples, cored and sliced
1 1-lb. can sweet potatoes, sliced
2 Tbsp. brown sugar
½ tsp. cinnamon
⅛ tsp. salt
⅛ tsp. black pepper
Grated rind of 1 lemon
1 cup apple juice

Preheat oven to 350 degrees. Layer apples and sweet
potatoes in greased casserole dish. Sprinkle with brown
sugar, cinnamon, salt and pepper. Top with lemon rind.
Pour apple juice evenly over top and bake for 30 minutes.
Makes 4 servings.

VARIATION: Instead of cinnamon, scatter cinnamon
red hot candies over top.

Coconut-Pecan Sweet Potato Slices

2 1-lb. packages sweet potato slices (8 per pkg.)
1 cup light brown sugar, packed
1 cup flaked coconut
1 cup chopped pecans
½ cup butter

Preheat oven to 350 degrees. Combine brown sugar,
coconut and pecans; cut in butter till crumbly. Place
sweet potato slices in lightly greased 9x13-inch baking
dish. Cover with crumb topping and bake till hot and
bubbly, about 20 minutes.
NOTE: McKenzie's sliced sweet potato slices are found
in the meat or refrigerator dept. of grocery store.

Nancy's Baked Corn

Nancy Barwick Crew sent me this recipe and said it was one of her family's favorite casseroles.

1 tube (1-lb. 4-oz) of frozen cream corn, thawed
2 large eggs, lightly beaten
2 Tbsp. sugar
½ cup plain yellow cornmeal
1 tsp. baking powder
¼ tsp. salt
¼ tsp. black pepper
½ cup milk
½ cup *each* Cheddar and Mozzerella, cheese, grated

Preheat oven to 375 degrees. Completely thaw corn; add eggs and sugar, mixing well. Combine cornmeal, baking powder, salt, and pepper and add to corn mixture. Stir in milk. Pour into greased 2-quart casserole, cover and bake until center is set, about 45 minutes. Remove from oven and cover top evenly with cheeses. Replace lid and set aside to allow cheese to melt from heat of corn.

Nellie Neel's Asparagus Casserole

4 Tbsp. butter
4 Tbsp. flour
1 tsp. salt
2 cups milk
1 cup grated sharp cheese
1 large can asparagus
Dash of red pepper
½ cup chopped almonds

Preheat oven to 300 degrees. Melt butter in saucepan, blend in flour and salt until smooth. Gradually stir in milk and cook over medium heat, stirring constantly until sauce becomes thickened and smooth. Stir in cheese and dash of red pepper, stirring until cheese is melted. Drain can of asparagus spears. Place in a 1-quart baking dish (8 or 9 inch pyrex). Pour sauce over asparagus, sprinkle with almonds and bake for 30 minutes. Makes 4-6 servings

Eggplant Ritz

1 medium eggplant, peeled and cut into cubes
3 large eggs, beaten
½ cup milk
½ cup butter
Salt & black pepper to taste
1½ cups grated cheddar cheese
2 cups Ritz cracker crumbs

Preheat oven to 350 degrees. Boil eggplant in water till fork tender; drain. Combine with eggs, milk, butter, salt and pepper. Pour into buttered 1½ qt. baking dish. Combine cheese and cracker crumbs and spread evenly on top. Bake for 30 minutes till top is golden brown. Makes 6-8 servings

Seasoned Green Beans

In the South, often called "snap beans" because they make a "snapping" sound when broken, by hand.

2 lbs. fresh young green beans
1 medium onion, chopped, about ¾ cup
2 to 3 Tbsp. bacon grease
2 cups Swanson's chicken broth
Water
6 to 8 slices of salt pork, 2 in. in length or 1 ham hock

Wash beans; cut off tips at stem ends and remove strings. Cut into 1½ inch pieces. Saute onion in a little bacon grease. Place beans, onions and broth in a 5 quart Dutch oven, adding enough water to cover beans. Stir a couple of times to mix; then bury the meat down in the middle of the beans. Bring to a boil, cover and cook on medium heat until beans are fork tender. Makes about 10-12 servings

Green Bean Casserole

Campbell Soup introduced this Casserole in the 1950's. It caught on instantly and became a "staple" on most southern Thanksgiving and Christmas dinner tables. It still is! When I cooked for Campbell's CEO, John Dorrance, we had it often!

2 10-oz. pkg. frozen cut green beans cooked & drained
1 10-oz. can cream of mushroom soup
½ cup milk
1 tsp. soy sauce
Dash of black pepper
1 3½ oz. can French fried onion rings

Preheat oven to 350 degrees. Combine soup, milk, soy sauce and black pepper. Mix in beans and ½ can onions. Place in 1½ qt .baking dish. Bake for 25 minutes; stir. Top with remaining onions. Bake 5 more minutes.

Option #1: French cut string beans can be used instead of cut green beans.
Option #2 Layer 1, 5-oz. can water chestnuts, drained and sliced, with the bean layer.

Granny's Green Bean Casserole Tips:

1. Best to use frozen or fresh green beans. If you do choose canned, use 2, 16 oz. cans, drained.
2. Sprinkle the onion rings on top *just* before baking to insure a crunchy topping.
3. You can make the casserole ahead and refrigerate till baking time. Leave off the topping until just before baking.

OYSTER CASSEROLE
Also called Scalloped Oysters

1 qt. fresh oysters
2 cups oyster crackers
¼ cup butter, melted
1 cup milk

1 tsp. Worcestershire
    sauce
½ tsp. salt
Black pepper to taste

Preheat ovent to 350 degrees. Drain oysters, reserving ½ cup liquor. Check for bits of shell. Toss oyster crackers with melted butter in a bowl. In a 1½ qt. baking dish, place a layer of crackers; then half of the oysters; sprinkle with salt & pepper. Combine the reserved oyster liquor with milk and Worcestershire sauce in a bowl, mixing well. Pour this liquid mixture over layers. Bake for 40 minutes. Makes 8 servings.
VARIATION; Substitute half-and-half or whipping cream for the milk, if desired.

GOURMET BROCCOLI
A smaller recipe with a different twist.

1 10-oz. pkg. frozen broccoli spears
¼ cup mayonnaise
⅓ cup sour cream
1 tsp. minced onion
⅛ tsp. cayenne pepper

Cook broccoli according to package directions. Drain, leaving broccoli in pan. Combine remaining ingredients and pour over broccoli and heat. Pour into a serving dish. No Baking! Makes 3-4 servings

LAYERED BROCCOLI CASSEROLE

2 10-oz. pkg. frozen chopped broccoli
1 10³/₄-oz. can cream of mushroom soup
2 Tbsp. grated onion
2 large eggs, slightly beaten
1 cup mayonnaise
1 cup grated cheddar cheese
1 cup Ritz cracker crumbs for topping

Cook broccoli just till fork tender; drain and cool. Place in bottom of a buttered 2-qt. baking dish. Combine rest of ingredients except cracker crumbs in a bowl, mixing well. Pour over broccoli. Top with cracker crumbs. Bake in preheated 350 degree oven for 40 minutes.
Makes 8-10 servings

CHEESY-SPINACH CASSEROLE

2 10-oz. pkg. frozen chopped spinach
1 10³/₄ oz. can cream of mushroom soup
1 4-oz.can sliced mushrooms
³/₄ cup grated sharp cheddar cheese
1 5-oz. can water chestnuts, drained & sliced
1 3½-oz. can French fried onion rings, crushed
5 slices bacon, fried crisp & crumbled

Preheat oven to 350 degrees. Cook spinach according to package directions and drain well. Place in 1-qt. casserole baking dish with soup, mushrooms, water chestnuts, cheese, ½ of the crushed onion rings, and all of the crumbled bacon. Cover and bake for 15 minutes. Uncover and top with remaining crushed onion rings. Bake for 5 to 10 minutes more until bubbly.
Makes 6 - 8 servings

Shopping Day Casserole

Put this together before leaving for Christmas shopping or the night before...refrigerate it..and bake it when you return. A one-dish meal!

4 chicken breasts, cooked & cut into bite-size pieces
1 2-oz. jar chopped pimientos, drained
1 10¾-oz. can cream of celery soup
1 16-oz. can french-style green beans, drained
1 cup mayonnaise
1 cup grated sharp cheese for topping

Preheat oven to 350 degrees. Mix all of the ingredients together except cheese in a large bowl and pour into a lightly greased 9x13-inch baking dish. Scatter cheese evenly over top and bake for 30 to 40 minutes.
Makes 6-8 servings

Spinach Quiche

Another good one dish meal...add a green salad & rolls.

1 10-oz. pkg. frozen chopped spinach, thawed and
    squeezed dry
1 bunch green onions, finely chopped
4 large eggs, beaten
1 16-oz. pkg. creamy cottage cheese
2 cups grated cheddar cheese
1 9-inch pie crust, baked or 9-inch quiche pan lined
    with pie pastry, baked

Preheat oven to 325 degrees. Lightly spray pie pan or quiche pan with cooking spray. Combine spinach, onions, beaten eggs and cottage cheese, mixing well. Pour into baked pie shell and bake for 35 to 40 minutes or until knife inserted in center is set. Makes 6-8 servings
OPTIONAL: Add 6 slices bacon, cooked crisp and crumbled to mixture before baking.

Seafood Casserole

Also called Hot Seafood Salad. This is a great luncheon or supper dish after a busy day of Christmas shopping. You can assemble it ahead, leaving off the potato chips, refrigerate it and when you return, add the topping and bake. I served it as lunch for a couple of friends with a tossed salad, Pillsbury crescent rolls and my cheese-cake for dessert.

1 lb. medium shrimp, unpeeled & uncooked
1 lb. crabmeat (or 2, 6-oz. cans, well drained & picked over for bits of shell)
1 cup maonnaise
1½ cups chopped celery hearts
½ cup chopped green bell pepper
½ cup chopped onions
Salt & black pepper to taste
2 Tbsp. lemon juice
1 tsp. Worcestershire sauce
2 cups crushed plain potato chips

Preheat oven to 375 degrees. Blanch shrimp for just one minute and peel. Blanching makes them easier to peel. Combine shrimp with rest of ingredients, *except potato chips*. (Drain canned crabmeat well, so casserole won't be "soupy") Pour into lightly greased 9x13-inch baking dish. Sprinkle potato chips evenly over top and bake for 30 minutes. Makes 8 servings.
NOTE: Don't buy cooked shrimp; over-cooking will make them tough. And don't buy frozen shrimp or your casserole will be "soupy".

Granny's Cooking Tip:

When substituting table salt for Kosher salt in a recipe, use ½ as much because table salt is saltier.

🆂ALADS....

Southerners *love* salads..... especially dessert-type salads.

At Christmastime we *must* have Waldorf Salad and don't forget that all-time favorite, "That Green Salad"! There must be at least 2 dozen variations of it.

In this section you'll find some all-time favorite holiday salads to choose from. I hope you find your own favorite or one your Grandma made for you every Christmas.

🅵RESH 🅲RANBERRY 🆂AUCE

2 cups sugar
2 cups water
1 16-oz. pkg. (4 cups) fresh cranberries
1 Tbsp. fresh orange zest
1 Tbsp. Cointreau or Triple Sec orange liqueur (optional)

Combine sugar and water in a medium saucepan; bring to a boil, stirring to dissolve sugar. Add cranberries, orange peel and liqueur. Cook till skins pop, about 5 or 10 minutes. Remove from heat; Serve warm or cover and chill till serving time. Makes 4 cups

CRANBERRY CHRISTMAS RING
Two beautiful layers, make this an all-time
Christmas favorite.

1st Layer:
1 6-oz. pkg. strawberry Jello
2 cups hot water
1 11-oz. jar cranberry relish
Dash of salt

Dissolve strawberry Jello in hot water; add cranberry
relish and salt. Pour into lightly greased large 8 cup
round ring mold, that measures 11x2 inches. Chill till firm.

2nd Layer:
1 20-oz can crushed pineapple, drained, reserve syrup
1 6-oz. pkg. lemon Jello
1¼ cups boiling water
4 cups miniature marshmallows
2 3-oz. pkgs. cream cheese, softened
1 cup mayonnaise
Dash of salt
1 cup whipping cream, whipped

Drain pineapple, reserving syrup. Dissolve lemon Jello in
boiling water; add marshmallows and stir till melted.
Add reserved pineapple syrup. Pour in a bowl and chill
until partially set. Beat cream cheese, mayonnaise and
salt together. Add to marshmallow mixture; stir in
pineapple. Fold in whipped cream. Pour over 1st layer
and refrigerate until firm. When ready to serve, turn
upside down on large serving plate. Surround with pretty lettuce leaves and put several leaves in center.
Makes about 20 to 22 servings.
NOTE: For a small 8 inch ring mold, halve the recipe,
using 1 cup of cranberry relish in the 1st layer.
Large copper ring molds can be found in kitchen shops.

Gail's Apple Custard Salad

1 14¼ oz. can Pineapple Tidbits
¾ cup sugar
2½ Tbsp. flour
3 large egg yolks
2 Tbsp. margarine
1 medium Red Delicious apple, unpeeled and cut up
1 cup miniature marshmallows
Chopped pecans (optional)

Drain pineapple tidbits, reserving syrup.
CUSTARD: To the syrup add sugar, flour and egg yolks.
Cook until thickened; add margarine. Remove from heat
and cool. Combine cut up apple, marshmallows and
reserved pineapple tidbits; carefully stir into custard
and add chopped pecans, if desired.
Makes 4-6 servings

Gail Whiddon
Thomasville, GA

Aunt Judy's Christmas Pears

In the fall when Aunt Judy and my Grandma canned
the pear halves, Aunt Judy always tinted a few jars for
her holiday meals. She put a few drops of red food
coloring in some jars and a few drops of green food
coloring in the other jars.

Granny Says:
If a congealed salad doesn't unmold easily,
turn it upside down on a serving plate and
place a very warm tea towel on the mold for
just a minute or two and gently shake it.

"That Green Salad"

This lime jello salad, which has been a holiday tradition in many families for at least 50 years, has as many names as it has recipes. I think men gave it it's name by referring to it as "That Green Salad".
You either love it or you hate it!

1 3-oz. pkg. lime gelatin
1 3-oz. pkg. lemon gelatin
2 cups boiling water
1 cup evaporated milk
2 Tbsp. lemon juice
1 lb. creamy-style cottage cheese
1 20-oz. can crushed pineapple, drained
1 20-oz. can crushed pineapple, drained
1 cup chopped walnuts
1 cup chopped celery

In a large bowl, combine both gelatins with the boiling water, stirring well to dissolve. Let cool to room temperature. Stir in evaporated milk and lemon juice. Chill in refrigerator until it is thick but *not* completely jelled, about 30 minutes.
Fold cottage cheese, pineapple, nuts and celery into the gelatin mixture, mixing well. Cover and refrigerate till it is completely set. To serve, cut into 15 squares

Heavenly Hash

2 3½-oz cans flaked coconut (2⅔ cups total)
1 20-oz. can crushed pineapple, undrained
1 6-oz. bottle red maraschino cherries, cut up
1 16-oz. pkg. miniature marshmallows
½ pt. whipping cream

Mix coconut, pineapple, cherries and marshmallows together. Let stand over-night in refrigerator. Whip cream and gently fold into fruit mixture. Chill.
Makes 12-14 servings

CHRISTMAS LIME SALAD
This one is in 2 pretty layers.

First Layer:
1¾ cups boiling water
1   3-oz. pkg. lime Jell-O
2   drops green food coloring

Dissolve Jell-O in the boiling water; add food coloring.
Pour in a 2-qt. pan and refrigerate till firm.

Second Layer:
1 8-oz. can crushed pineapple,   1 cup evaporated milk
     reserve syrup   ½ cup chopped celery
1 3-oz. pkg. lime Jell-O   hearts
1 Tbsp. lemon juice   ½ cup chopped pecans

Drain pineapple and add enough water to reserved syrup
to equal one cup. Bring this liquid to a boil and pour over
Jell-O, stirring to dissolve. Add lemon juice and evaporated milk. Fold in celery and pecans. Pour over the congealed 1st layer. Refrigerate till firm. Cut in squares to
serve.

SIX-CUP SALAD

1 cup mandarin oranges   1 cup shredded coconut
1 cup maraschino cherries   1 cup chopped pecans
1 cup mini marshmallows   1 cup dairy sour cream

Mix all together and refrigerate overnight.
Makes 8 servings

VARIATION: Add or substitute: 16-oz can fruit cocktail,
pineapple chunks or seedless green grapes.

Waldorf Salad

No Southern Christmas dinner is complete without this.
It doubles & triples easily.

4 Red Delicious apples, unpeeled and diced
1 Tbsp. lemon juice
1 cup diced celery
1 cup red or green seedless grapes, halved
1 cup miniature marshmallows
¼ cup mayonnaise
¼ cup whipping cream, whipped
1 cup chopped pecans or walnuts

Sprinkle apples with lemon juice to keep them from turning dark. Combine celery, grapes, marshmallows and mayonnaise. Fold in whipped cream. Just before serving add nuts. Serve in a pretty glass bowl or lettuce-lined bowl. Makes 6 servings.
NOTE: Apple Cider may be substituted for the lemon juice.

Apple Salad

A simple waldorf salad

4 medium Red Delicious apples, unpeeled, chopped
2 ribs celery hearts, chopped
1 cup seedless purple grapes, halved
1 cup chopped pecans or walnuts
½ cup or more if needed, mayonnaise or salad dressing

Mix all together. Makes about 2 quarts
NOTE: 1 cup of dark or light raisins can be substituted for the grapes.

Yum Yum Salad

1 3-oz. pkg. orange gelatin
1 cup boiling water
1 cup cold water
1 cup mandarin oranges
1 cup whipping cream, whipped

Combine Jell-O in boiling water; add cold water.
Chill until *partially* set; add oranges. Place in sherbet
glasses and top with whipped cream.
Makes 4 servings

Mr. G's Pickles

A great side for your Holiday dinner or as gifts!
From our good friend, Milton Gerock, Wilmington, NC

1 gallon jar big dill pickles   **Whole garlic cloves**
5 lbs. sugar

Drain pickles and discard juice. Slice the pickles into
rounds, about ¼ inch thick. Starting at the bottom of
the same gallon jar, put a layer of pickle slices, a layer of
sugar (about 1 cup) and 2 garlic cloves. Repeat all the
way to the top. Then, every day for 3 weeks, turn the jar
upside down, then right side up. When ready to give as
gifts, spoon pickles out into pint jar with a little juice
and a garlic clove. Decorate top of jar with a square of
country-style fabric tied with a ribbon, raffia, or fat
yarn.
NOTE: You can cut the fabric with pinking shears or just
tear it for the country look. No sewing needed!

Frozen Fruit Salad

2 3-oz. pkg. cream cheese, softened
1 cup mayonnaise
¼ cup lemon juice
1 15-oz can fruit cocktail, drained
1 4-oz jar maraschino cherries, chopped
1 cup chopped pecans
½ pt. whipping cream, whipped

Combine cream cheese, mayonnaise and lemon juice, beating till smooth. In a separate bowl, combine fruit cocktail, chopped cherries, drained, but use a small amount of juice for color. Add to cream cheese mixture; add pecans. Fold in whipped cream and pour in 2-qt. pan and freeze. Cut in squares, place on lettuce leaf and dab a little mayo on each square and top with whole cherry. Makes 8-10 servings

Cooked Salad Dressing

This is a nice old fashioned cooked salad dressing to serve on the side of a fruit salad.

½ cup pineapple juice
3 Tbsp. lemon juice
½ cup sugar

1½ Tbsp. flour
2 large eggs, beaten
¼ cup water

Combine all in top of double boiler. Cook, stirring constantly with a wooden spoon until slightly thickened. Cool and serve on side with fruit salad.
Makes 4-6 servings

Apricot Congealed Salad

FIRST LAYER:
1 6-oz. pkg. apricot Jell-O
2 cups boiling water
2 cups cold water
2 bananas, sliced
1 cup miniature marshmallows
1 20-oz. can crushed pineapple, drained, reserve juice

Mix all of the above ingredients together. Refrigerate to congeal. You'll use the reserved juice for the 2nd layer.

SECOND LAYER: (topping)
2 Tbsp. butter
½ cup sugar
½ cup of the reserved pineapple juice
2 Tbsp. flour
1 envelope Dream Whip
1 8-oz. pkg. cream cheese, softened
½ cup chopped pecans

Combine the butter, sugar, reserved pineapple juice and flour in top of double boiler and over simmering wafer, cook until thick.
Prepare the envelope of Dream Whip as directed on package. Add softened cream cheese and beat with electric mixer on high for 2 minutes.
Fold into the cooked topping and spread on congealed first layer.
Sprinkle chopped pecans evenly over top.

Granny Says:
I don't like health foods. At my age,
I need all the preservatives I can get!

ℙOTATO-⊛NION 𝒮ALAD

6 medium-size potatoes
1 large yellow onion, thinly sliced and separated into
      rings
Oil-Vinegar Marinade (recipe follows)
1 green bell pepper (for garnish)

Wash and cook potatoes for about 20 to 30 minutes or
until tender when pierce with fork; drain and dry by shaking in pan over low heat. Set aside to cool. Peel cooled
potatoes, cut into ¼ inch slices. Arrange potatoes and
onion rings alternately in large shallow bowl;
add Oil-Vinear Marinade. Chill for at least 1 hour in
refrigerator, carefully turning vegetables occasionly.

OIL-VINEGAR MARINADE:

½ cup cider vinegar
2 Tbsp. oil (olive or vegetable)
1 Tbsp. sugar
1 tsp. salt
½ tsp. black pepper

Place all ingredients into small screw-top jar; cover
tightly. Shake until blended. Store in refrigerator;
shake well before using

TO SERVE: Pour marinade off potatoes and onions
before serving; garnish salad with pepper rings.
Makes about 6 servings. Easily doubled or tripled.

Bell Pepper Garnish:
Rinse and remove stem end off of bell pepper, shortly
before serving. Also remove white fiber and seeds; rinse
inside and cut crosswise into ⅛-inch rings.; set aside.

(If there had been three wise women instead of three wise men):

Three Wise Women...
Would have:
Asked for directions,
Arrived on time,
Helped deliver the baby,
Cleaned the stable,
Made a casserole
and
Brought practical gifts:
Then, there would be
Peace on Earth

Author Unknown

Away in a Manger

Although the authorship of this beautiful and melodic hymn is sometimes credited to Martin Luther, there is no proof that he wrote it. It is, however, a 15th Century carol of German origin. A charming composition, its gently flowing melody and lullaby-like rhythm seem to suggest the rocking of a cradle.

MARTIN LUTHER (?)

GERMAN
Arranged by Ruth Heller

Tenderly

1. A - way in a man - ger, no crib for His bed, The lit - tle Lord Je - sus laid down His sweet head. The stars in the sky, — looked down where He lay, The lit - tle Lord Je - sus a - sleep in the hay.

2. The cat - tle are low - ing, the poor Ba - by wakes, But lit - tle Lord Je - sus, no cry - ing He makes; I love Thee, Lord Je - sus, look down from the sky, And stay by my cra - dle till morn - ing is nigh.

Loo, loo, loo, loo, loo, loo, loo, Loo, loo, — loo, loo, loo, loo, loo, loo, Loo, loo, loo, loo, loo, loo, loo, loo, Loo, loo, loo, loo, — loo, Loo, — loo, loo.

Holiday Breads
& Pastries

Merry Christmas to all, and to all a good night!

RECIPES

Extra:

Granny's Gooey Christmas Buns

A delicious fun and easier "Monkey Bread" made with frozen rolls instead of biscuits. Perfect for Christmas morning because you put it together the night before and bake it in the morning.

1   cup chopped pecans
18 frozen Rhodes frozen rolls
1   3-oz. pkg. cook & serve vanilla or butterscotch
     pudding mix (not instant)
½   cup butter
¾   cup light brown sugar
1   tsp. cinnamon

Butter a Bundt or Tube pan well. Sprinkle pecans evenly over bottom. Arrange frozen rolls in pan and pour dry pudding mix over rolls. Bring butter, brown sugar and cinnamon to a boil, reduce to low and boil for 1 minute. Pour over rolls. Leave on the counter to rise overnight. Do not cover. Next morning, preheat oven to 350 degrees and bake rolls for 30 minutes. Let stand 10 minutes and then invert onto large, lightly buttered serving plate.

OPTIONAL: For a mid-morning brunch, you *could* cover the pan of unbaked prepared rolls and let rise at room temperature for 3 hours. Then bake, uncovered, on the lower oven rack at 350 degrees for 30 minutes. Just choose the option you prefer.

NOTE: Rhodes frozen rolls come in a 1-lb., 12 count bag or a 3-lb., 36 count bag in the freezer section of the grocery.

Homemade by
Miss Dee's Kitchen

APPLE STRUDEL

1 cup butter, cold
2 cups flour
3 large egg yolks

2 Tbsp. apple cider vinegar
¼ cup water

Cut butter into flour as for pie pastry; add egg yolks, vinegar and water. Mix well; cover. Refrigerate overnight. Next day: divide dough into 3 parts; roll each part out into a 10x15-inch rectangle, one at a time, on a lightly floured cloth. Follow directions for filling.

FILLING:
3 Tbsp. flour
9 Tbsp. sugar
1½ tsp. ground cinnamon

9 cooking apples, peeled,
    cored and diced

Preheat oven to 375 degrees. Mix *1* tablespoon flour, *3* tablespoons sugar, *½ tsp.* cinnamon for *each* rectangle. Sprinkle over top. Arrange *⅓* of the diced apples along edge of long side; roll up. Place on greased pan. *Repeat* with other 2 doughs.
Bake for 45 minutes. Makes 3 strudels

CHRISTMAS STOLLEN

A German fruit bread that is traditionally folded over
but is much prettier braided.

1½ **cups milk**
2 **(¼-oz. each) pkg. dry yeast**
2 **cups all-purpose flour**
¼ **cup sugar**

Heat milk to lukewarm; stir in yeast. Combine this mixture with the flour and sugar. Stir well. This is the
"sponge". Let it sit till it is bubbly, about 15 minutes.

6 **large eggs**   2 **tsp. grated lemon**
1 **cup butter, softened**   1 to 1½ **cups candied**
½ **tsp. ground cardamom**   **fruit & raisins**
2 **tsp. salt**   5 **cups flour**

When the sponge is bubbly, add the above ingredients,
adding the flour 1 cup at a time. Knead until smooth
and shiny. If it is sticky, add a little bit more flour, but
not very much. Place in a greased bowl, turning the
dough over so the top of the dough is greased. This is
so it won't form a crust. Let rise in a draft-free place
till doubled. (I find the microwave good for this because
it is air-tight) When risen, punch dough down and
divide into 4 to 6 pieces. Divide each piece into 3
pieces. With your hands, roll each piece into a long rope
about 6 to 9 inches long. Braid these pieces, tucking
under the ends. Place on greased baking sheet and let
rise till almost double. Brush with a mixture of 1 beaten
egg and 1 tablespoon water; top with blanched almonds.
Bake 350 degrees for 25 to 30 minutes till golden.
Cool and sprinkle each stollen generously with powdered
sugar. Or mix 1 cup sifted powdered sugar and 2 Tbsp.
hot water and drizzle over loaves.
NOTE: Cardamom is related to ginger, a little spicy.

CHRISTMAS BREAKFAST SOPAIPILLAS

2 cups flour
1 tsp. salt
2 tsp. baking powder

2 tsp. shortening
½ cup buttermilk
½ cup water

Combine flour, salt and baking powder; cut in shortening as for biscuit dough until well blended. Add buttermilk and water, kneading until dough can be easily handled. Form dough into 4 balls. Roll each ball out on a lightly floured surface into a rectangle, about 5"x3"x¼" thick. Cut into squares to resemble "little pillows", (which is where the word comes from). Heat 3 inches of vegetable oil to 375 degrees. Drop a few pieces of dough at a time, depending on the size of the pan. They will instantly rise to the top. Fry about 1½ minutes, until evenly brown, turning once. Drain on paper towels. Serve hot with honey on the side or cover generously with powdered sugar. Makes 16

EASY FRIED BISCUIT DONUTS

Over the years, I've made a "zillion" of these, on Sunday mornings. They're almost too simple to call a "recipe"!

Canned biscuits, regular type, not the "flaky layers"
Vegetable oil to fry
Cinnamon-sugar

Heat about 3 inches of oil in frying pan. Cut a hole in the center of each biscuit with a small bottle cap, (like vanilla extract) or stretch a hole in center with fingers. Carefully slide biscuits and holes in oil and fry on each side a couple of minutes, turning once, till golden brown. Drain on paper towels. Put cinnamon-sugar in a paper bag and drop a few biscuits and holes at a time into the bag and shake vigorously to coat. Serve hot.

POTATO DONUTS
Also called "Spud Nuts"

1 ¼-oz. pkg. active dry yeast
½ cup warm water
1 tsp. salt
½ cup sugar
⅔ cup shortening
2 cups scalded milk
1 cup mashed potatoes, unseasoned
2 large eggs, beaten

6 to 7 cups flour
2 cups powdered sugar
1 tsp. vanilla

Add yeast to water. Add salt, sugar and shortening to scalded milk; cool. Add unseasoned mashed potatoes, eggs, yeast and flour. Roll out dough and cut into 1½ inch rounds, no holes. Let dough rise for 1 hour. Fry in shortening at 350 degrees until brown, turning once. Drain on paper towels.
Combine powdered sugar and vanilla and a little bit of water to make a smooth glaze. Dip donuts in glaze and place on wire rack to dry. Makes 60 servings.

CREAM CHEESE ICING
This is a nice easy little frosting that is great for donuts, cinnamon rolls, muffin tops, etc.

4 oz. cream cheese, softened (½ of 8-oz. pkg.)
¼ cup butter, softened
1 cup sifted powdered sugar
1 tsp. vanilla
1½ tsp. milk

Beat with electric beaters till smooth. Makes about 2 cups

Amish Friendship Bread

STARTER:
1   1/4-oz. pkg. dry yeast
1/4   cup warm water
3   cups all-purpose flour, divided
3   cups granulated sugar, divided
3   cups milk

Directions:
In a small bowl, dissolve yeast in water. Let stand 10 minutes. In a 2 quart container, glass, plastic or ceramic, combine *1 cup flour and 1 cup sugar*. Mix thoroughly or flour will lump when milk is added. Slowly stir in *1 cup milk* and dissolved yeast mixture. Cover loosely and let stand at room temperature until bubbly.
This is the 1st day of the 10 day cycle.
Days 2 through 4: Stir starter with a wooden spoon.
Day 5: Stir in 1 cup of flour, 1 cup sugar and 1 cup milk.
Days 6 through 9: Stir only.
Day 10: Stir in 1 cup flour, 1 cup sugar and 1 cup milk. Remove 1 cup to make your first loaf and give away 2 cups to friends along with this recipe. Store the remaining 1 cup starter in a container in the refrigerator.
You can also freeze these starters in 1 cup measurements for later use. When ready to use, bring to room temperature before using.

BREAD RECIPE: This recipe makes 2 loaves
1   cup starter
1/2   cup oil
1/2   cup applesauce
1   cup granulated sugar
1   tsp. vanilla
3   large eggs
1/2   cup milk   Continued:

220

Continued:
2 cups bread flour
1½ tsp. baking powder
½ tsp. baking soda
½ tsp. salt
2 tsp. ground cinnamon
1 5.1-oz. pkg. instant vanilla pudding mix
1 cup chopped pecans or walnuts
½ cup golden raisins
½ cup chopped dates

Preheat oven to 325 degrees. Combine starter, oil, applesauce, sugar, vanilla, eggs and milk. In another bowl, combine flour, baking powder, baking soda, salt and cinnamon; add to starter mixture. Add dry pudding mix. Fold in nuts, raisins and dates. Pour evenly into 2 greased and floured 9X5-inch loaf pans. Bake for 60 minutes till straw inserted in center comes out clean. Cool in pans 10 minutes before removing to wire rack to cool completely.

The Pennsylvania Amish meet in members' homes for their church services. During the week, before their service on Sunday, all of the benches are transported to the designated home where the worship service will be held.

Tracey's Friendship Bread

Daughter Tracey passed this on to me years ago when she was given a cup of starter by a friend. Make it in gift size loaves, put in plastic bags (not the zip kind), tie a piece of fat yarn around the top and add your own hand written label and instructions. Don't forget to add a cup of the starter!

STARTER:
1 cup warm water
½ cup sugar
1 ¼-oz. pkg. active dry yeast (2¼ tsp.)
3 Tbsp. instant potato flakes

Combine starter ingredients, mixing well. Let stand at room temperature to allow fermentation for 2 days. Then feed with the following Starter Feeder.

STARTER FEEDER:
1 cup warm water
½ cup sugar
3 Tbsp. instant potato flakes

Mix well; add to starter. Let stand at room temperature for 8 hours. Mixture will be very bubbly. Take out one cup to make bread and put the remainder, covered loosely, in the refrigerator. Feed again in 3 to 5 days. *Important*: If not making bread after feeding the starter, discard *one cup*. This is to avoid deflating the starter. Keep container closed but not too tight or it might explode!

TO MAKE BREAD TWICE A WEEK:

1. Feed starter on Monday AM, mix dough on Monday night. Make bread on Tuesday.

Continued:

Continued:

2. Feed starter on Thursday AM, mix dough on Thursday night. Make bread on Friday.   :

NOTE: Bread flour should be used.

BREAD RECIPE:
¼ cup sugar	⅓ cup corn oil
1 Tbsp. salt	1½ cups warm water
6 cups bread flour	1 cup starter

Combine the above ingredients, making a stiff batter.
Knead for 5 to 10 minutes on a floured surface.
If you have a mixer with a dough hook, let it do this step
for you, kneading only for about 4 minutes
Put dough in a greased bowl, turning over once to grease
all sides. Cover with a damp dish cloth and let sit
overnight.
Next morning: Punch dough down and knead a little on a
floured surface. Divide dough into or 2, 9-inch size
loaves and place in greased loaf pans. Covered lightly
and let rise 6 to 8 hours till doubled.
Bake at 350 degrees for 25 to 30 minutes.

NOTE: 2 easy ways to let dough rise:
1. Place a very hot bowl of water on the oven rack below
the rack on which the dough is to be placed.
The moisture helps in the rising.

2. Heat a cup of water in the microwave for one minute.
Then place the dough, lightly covered, in the microwave.
Again the moisture helps. Of course, do not turn the
microwave back on!

Date Nut Gift Breads

1 cup chopped dates
2 cups boiling water
2 tsp. baking soda
2 Tbsp. butter
2 cups sugar

2 large eggs
2 tsp. vanilla
4 cups flour
1 cup chopped nuts

Combine dates, water and baking soda; let cool. Mix butter, sugar and eggs together; add date mixture, vanilla, flour and nuts. Fill 5 or 6 greased cans** ½ full. Bake at 350 degrees for 1 hour.
** Good source for baking cans: Crushed pineapple comes in #20 size cans, which is 2½ cups. I would suggest saving these cans during the year for your holiday gift breads.

Orange Pecan Bread

2 cups flour
½ cup sugar
1 tsp. salt
1 tsp. baking soda
1 large egg, beaten

¼ cup butter, melted
1 tsp. grated orange peel
1 tsp. grated lemon peel
1 cup orange juice
1 cup chopped pecans

Preheat oven to 350 degrees. Combine flour, sugar, salt and baking soda together. Add the rest of the ingredients and mix well. Pour into a well greased 9-inch loaf pan. Cover and let rise at room temperature for 15 minutes. Then bake for 50 minutes. Makes 1, 9-inch loaf

ICING:
Sift **1 cup powdered sugar; add about 1 tablespoon or less, orange juice.** Drizzle over top of warm bread. Sprinkle a few finely **chopped pecans** on top.
Thinned, it will be a *glaze,* thick, it will be more like *icing.*

Pennsylvania Funnel Cakes

This recipe makes 6 funnel cakes. To make more, just double batter. Make for breakfast instead of pancakes!

1 cup flour	1/8 tsp. salt
1/4 cup milk	1 large egg
1 tsp. baking powder	Powdered sugar

In a 12-inch skillet heat 4 cups salad oil over medium heat to 370 degrees. With wire whisk stir the flour, milk, baking powder, salt and egg together till smooth. Pour about 1/4 cup batter into a narrow spouted funnel with 1/2 inch spout. Holding your finger over the end, carefully remove finger to let batter run out in a steady stream, making a spiral about 6 inches in diameter. The funnel cake will puff up and float. Let fry for about 6 to 8 minutes, till golden brown, turning only once. Drain well on paper towels and sift powdered sugar generously over top. Serve hot. Repeat with remaining batter, stirring well. Makes 6 funnel cakes.

Amish children playfully climb the fence after the church meeting. When they saw me taking their picture, they snatched their hats off and held them in front of their faces!

CREAM CHEESE DANISH
An easy Christmas morning treat!

2 8-oz. cans crescent rolls
2 8-oz. pkg. cream softened
1 cup sugar
1 large egg, separated
1 tsp. vanilla
1 cup pecans, chopped
Powdered sugar

Preheat oven to 375 degrees. Unroll 1 can of the rolls and press into a lightly greased 9x13-inch baking dish, sealing edges and perforations. Beat cream cheese with sugar, egg yolk and vanilla until smooth and creamy. Spread evenly over crescent dough in pan. Unroll the 2nd can on a sheet of waxed paper and press into a 9x13-inch rectangle. Place over cream cheese mixture. Whisk the egg white; brush over roll dough and sprinkle with pecans. Bake for 25 minutes. Sprinkle with powdered sugar. Cool in pan placed on wire rack. Cut into squares. Makes 15-20 servings.

14-KARAT MUFFINS
For a Christmas morning crowd

2 cups flour
2 tsp. baking powder
2½ tsp. baking soda
1 tsp. salt
2 tsp. cinnamon
2 cups sugar
1½ cups oil

4 large eggs
2 cups grated carrots
1 cup drained, crushed
      pineapple
1/2 cup chopped nuts,
      walnuts or pecans

Continued:

Continued:
 Preheat oven to 350 degrees. Sift flour, baking powder, baking soda, salt and cinnamon together; add sugar and oil, mixing well. Beat in eggs; add carrots, pineapple and nuts. Spoon into 24 greased muffin tins. Bake for 30 minutes or till tested done with a toothpick. Cool and frost with Cream Cheese Frosting on page 219. OPTIONAL: Bak e 48 miniature muffins instead of 24 regular size for your Christmas morning Brunch. Bake in preheated 375 degree oven for about 15 minutes.

$\mathcal{A}$PPLE $\mathcal{B}$ROWN $\mathcal{B}$ETTY
A Granny's kitchen classic!

6 slices bread (or equal amount cinnamon rolls)
6 cups peeled, cored and sliced cooking apples
3/4 cup light brown sugar
1/2 tsp. cinnamon
1/4 tsp. salt
1/2 cup water
3/4 cup butter, melted

Preheat oven to 350 degrees. Break bread or rolls into small equal-sized crumbs. Toast slightly, stirring often, in shallow pan. Put 1/3 of the crumbs into a buttered 9-inch square baking pan. Cover crumbs with 1/2 of the apple slices. Mix the brown sugar, cinnamon and salt together and sprinkle 1/2 of this mixture over the apples. Repeat these layers. Top with the remaining 1/3 of the crumbs. Pour the water evenly over top and drizzle the melted butter over top. Cover with foil and bake for 30 minutes. Remove foil and bake for an additional 15 minutes. Serve warm with whipped cream.
Makes about 6 servings.
NOTE: A good way to use stale bread or raisin bread purchased from the bakery thrift store.

Sour Cream Coffeecake

A nice simple coffeecake. A good addition to a brunch or breakfast buffet

6 large eggs, beaten
2 cups sour cream
2 cups sifted flour
2 cups sugar
2 tsp. baking powder

½ tsp. baking soda
¼ tsp salt
⅓ cup brown sugar
1 tsp. cinnamon
½ cup chopped pecans

Preheat oven to 350 degrees. Combine lightly beaten eggs and sour cream. Sift flour and resift with sugar, baking powder, baking soda and salt. Add to egg mixture and beat until smooth, Spread dough in a greased 9x13 inch baking dish. Combine brown sugar, cinnamon and pecans and sprinkle evenly over top. Bake for 30 to 35 minutes. Cut into 12 squares and serve warm.

Blueberry Muffins

2 cups cake flour, sifted
⅔ cup sugar
1 Tbsp. baking powder
½ tsp. salt
1 tsp. nutmeg

2 large eggs
1 cup milk
⅓ cup melted butter
1 tsp. vanilla
2 cups fresh blueberries

Preheat oven to 375 degrees. Combine first 5 ingredients. In a separate bowl, combine eggs, milk, butter, and vanilla. Fold flour mixture into wet mixture just until moistened. Fold in blueberries. Fill greased muffin tins almost to the top. It will not spill over when baking. Bake for about 20 minutes. Leave in pan 5 minutes before turning out. Makes 12 regular size muffins

VARIATION: This will make 6 jumbo, "mall-muffins" (3½ inch).Bake at 375 for 20 to 25 minutes. Great taste!

6-Weeks Bran Muffins

A rage in the 1970's, so named because the batter could be kept in refrigerator as long as 6 weeks and you could take out as much as you wanted to bake at one time, leaving the rest covered tightly in the refrigerator.

1 15-oz. box Raisin Bran cereal
5 cups all-purpose flour
3 cups sugar
5 tsp. baking soda
2 tsp. salt
4 large eggs, beaten
1 qt. buttermilk
1 cup corn oil

Combine first 5 ingredients in a very large bowl; make a well in center and add eggs, buttermilk and oil; stir just enough to moisten dry ingredients. Cover tightly and store in refrigerator until ready to bake.

When ready to bake, spoon batter into greased muffin tins, filling ⅔ full. Bake at 400 degrees for 12 to 15 minutes. Makes about 5½ dozen

OVEN TEMPERATURE CHART FOR BREADS

Breads	Temperature	Time (minutes)
Loaf	350-400	50-60
Rolls	400-450	20-30
Biscuits	400-450	12-15
Muffins	375-450	20-25
Popovers	425-450	30-40
Cornbread	400-425	25-30
Nut Bread	350	50-75
Gingerbread	350-370	40-50

RASPBERRY-CHEESE COFFEECAKE

Make this in a 10 inch quiche pan, springform pan or 10-inch pie plate. It's sooo good!

2¼ cups flour
¾ cup sugar
¾ cup butter
½ tsp. baking soda
½ tsp. baking powder
¼ tsp. salt
¾ cup dairy sour cream
1 large egg
1 tsp. almond extract
1 8-oz. pkg. cream cheese softened
¼ cup sugar
1 large egg
½ cup raspberry preserves
¾ cup sliced almonds

CRUST:

Combine flour, and ¾ cup sugar; cut in butter with pastry cutter or 2 knives till crumbly. Set aside 1 cup of this crumb mixture.

FILLING:

To the remaining crumb mixture, add baking soda, baking powder, salt, sour cream, 1 egg, and almond extract. Spread batter over crust and 2 inches up sides of pan.

In another bowl combine softened cream cheese, ¼ cup sugar and 1 egg, blending well. Pour over batter.

Carefully spread preserves evenly over top. Sprinkle reserved crumb mixture over preserves. Scatter sliced almonds over top.

Bake at 350 degrees for 45 minutes or until cream cheese is set and top is golden brown. Cool slightly but serve warm.

Granny Wisdom:

Raising teenagers is like nailing Jell-o to a tree!

Sour Cream Coffeecake #2

Another great tasting simple coffeecake. Take this one to the office!

CAKE:

½ cup butter
1 cup sugar
2 large eggs
2 cups flour
1 tsp. baking soda

1 tsp. baking powder
½ tsp. salt
1 cup sour cream
1 tsp. vanilla

Preheat oven to 325 degrees. Cream butter and sugar together. Add eggs, one at a time, beating well after each addition. Sift flour, baking soda, baking powder and salt together. Add alternately with sour cream, beginning and ending with flour mixture. Stir in vanilla. Pour ½ of the batter in a buttered 9x13 inch baking dish. Cover with ½ of the topping mixture. Cover with other half of batter and top with the remaining half of topping. Bake for 40 minutes, till center tests done with a toothpick. Makes 10-12 servings

TOPPING:

Mix together:
⅓ cup light brown sugar
¼ cup granulated sugar

1 tsp. cinnamon
¼ cup chopped pecans

Apple Dumplings In Cheese Pastry

PASTRY:
1½ cup flour
1 tsp. salt
½ cup shortening
½ cup grated cheese, medium or sharp
Cold water

4 to 6 apples, peeled & cored
1 tsp. cinnamon
¼ cup sugar

Sift flour with salt. Cut in shortening and grated cheese. Add enough cold water to make a firm dough. Roll out and cut in squares large enough to cover apples. Combine one teaspoon cinnamon and ¼ cup sugar. Fill cavity of apples with mixture. Draw corners of dough squares up over apples; pinch together. Bake in 350 degree oven until apples are tender and crust slightly browned.

CINNAMON SAUCE:
1 cup sugar
2 Tbsp. butter
¾ cup water
1 tsp. cinnamon

Mix the sauce ingredients together in saucepan. Bring to a boil and boil for 5 minutes. Cool. When serving the apple dumplings, pour sauce over each apple.
GARNISH: Sprinkle top with additional grated cheese

Banana Nut Bread

½ cup butter
1 cup sugar
1 cup mashed ripe bananas
3 Tbsp. buttermilk
3 medium-size eggs

¼ tsp. salt
2 cups flour, sifted
1 tsp. baking soda
2 Tbsp. warm water
1 cup chopped pecans

Preheat oven to 325 degrees. Cream butter and sugar together; add bananas and buttermilk. Lightly beat eggs and stir into banana mixture. Add salt to sifted flour; sift again; stir into banana mixture. Dissolve baking soda in warm water and add. Stir in pecans.
Pour into greased 9x5x3-inch loaf pan. Bake for 55 minutes or until tested done. Store 24 hours before slicing. This is called letting it "ripen".
Serve with butter or softened cream cheese.

Banana Cake Bread
A holiday cake mix helper

1 18.25 oz. pkg. banana cake mix
1 ripe banana, mashed
½ cup flour
½ cup chopped nuts

Preheat oven to 400 degrees. Prepare cake mix according to package directions. Stir in mashed banana, flour and nuts. Pour into 2 greased 9x5x3-inch loaf pans. Bake for 50 to 60 minutes, testing done in center with straw.

CRANBERRY BREAD
Make turkey sandwiches out of this Christmas bread!

1½ cups chopped raw cranberries
4 tsp. grated orange peel
3 Tbsp. sugar
3 cups sifted all-purpose flour
3 tsp. baking powder
½ tsp. baking soda
¾ tsp. salt
¾ tsp. nutmeg
1¼ cups sugar
2 large eggs, beaten
¾ cup orange juice
¾ cup water
½ cup melted shortening
1 cup chopped walnuts

Preheat oven to 350 degrees.
Combine cranberries, orange peel and 3 tbsp. sugar; mix well and set aside.
Sift together the flour, baking powder, baking soda, salt, nutmeg and 1¼ cups sugar.
In a separate bowl combine eggs, orange juice and water, mixing well. Stir this mixture along with the melted shortening and cranberry mixture to the flour mixture, stirring just enough to moisten dry ingredients. Fold in nuts. Spoon into a greased 9x5 inch loaf pan.
Bake for 1 hour and 30 minutes or until toothpick inserted in center comes out clean. Leaving bread in pan, place on wire cooling rack for 20 minutes. Then turn out of pan and let cool completely on wire cooling rack.
Wrap bread in plastic wrap, place in refrigerator and let "ripen" for 24 hours. Then slice and enjoy!

Amish Friendship Cinnamon Bread

1 cup Friendship Bread Starter, p. 220
1 cup vegetable oil
1 cup granulated sugar
4 large eggs
2 tsp. vanilla
2 cups flour
2 tsp. baking soda
1 tsp. baking powder
1 3-oz. pkg. instant vanilla pudding mix
2 tsp. cinnamon
1 cup chopped pecans
1 cup light or dark raisins

The starter recipe on page 236 makes 3 cups. Use one cup for this recipe and freeze the remaining 2 cups, in 1 cup portions for later use.

Preheat oven to 325 degrees. Combine 1 cup of the starter, oil, sugar, eggs and vanilla, mixing well. In a separate bowl, combine flour, baking soda, baking powder, dry pudding mix and cinnamon; add to the starter mixture, beating well with a wooden spoon. Stir in pecans and raisins. Divide batter evenly into 3 well-greased 9-inch loaf pans and bake for 1 hour. Turn out immediately onto wire racks to cool. When cool, beat icing ingredients with electric beaters till smooth and spread on top. When icing is set and dry, slip loaves into 1 qt. plastic bags and tie with pretty red fat yarn for gifts.

CREAM CHEESE ICING:
4-oz. cream cheese, softened (½ of an 8 oz. pkg.)
¼ cup butter, softened
1 cup sifted powdered sugar
1 tsp. vanilla
1½ tsp. milk

✪LD-FASHIONED JELLY ROLL
Grandma made lots of these!

¾ cup sifted cake flour
1 tsp. baking powder
¼ tsp. salt
4 large eggs, room temperature
¾ cup sugar
1 tsp. vanilla
Powdered sugar, sifted
1 cup jelly, your choice

Preheat oven to 400 degrees. Sift flour, measure; set aside. Combine baking powder salt and eggs. Add sugar, beating until mixture becomes thick and light colored. Fold in flour and vanilla. Spread into a greased waxed paper lined 15x10-in jelly roll pan. Bake for 13 minutes. Turn cake out onto a towel that has been dusted with powdered sugar. Remove paper and cut crisp edges off of cake. Then roll cake *with towel* together from the 10-inch (short side). Cool 10 minutes; unroll. Spread with your choice of jelly. Roll up again, this time without the towel. Place on serving platter, seam side down and sprinkle generously with powdered sugar.
Makes 8 servings

©1995 Delafield Stamp Company

Spiced Apple Roll

2 cups Bisquick
³/₄ cup milk
1 cup chopped apples
½ cup water

½ tsp. cinnamon
½ sugar
2 Tbsp. butter

Preheat oven to 375 degrees. Combine Bisquick and milk; roll out dough on lightly floured surface to ¼ inch thickness. Spoon the apples evenly over dough. Roll up as for cinnamon rolls. Place cut side down into buttered 9-inch round baking pan. Combine cinnamon, sugar and butter with the water and bring to a boil. Pour mixture over rolls in pan. Bake for 35 to 40 minutes. Makes about 5 to 6 rolls

Zucchini Gift Bread

3 large eggs, beaten
2 cups sugar
1 cup oil
3 tsp. vanilla
3 cups flour
1 tsp. salt

1 tsp. baking soda
1 tsp. baking powder
3 tsp. cinnamon
2 cups grated zucchini, unpeeled
1 cup chopped pecans

Preheat oven to 325 degrees. To the beaten eggs, add sugar, oil and vanilla. Beat well. Sift dry ingredients together; add to egg mixture. Stir in zucchini and nuts. Spoon into 2 greased 9-inch loaf pans and bake for 1 hour. Makes 2 loaves

NOTE: Instead of 2, 9-inch loaves, you can make 3, 7-inch loaves and bake for about 45 minutes.. Place bread in quart-size plastic bags and tie top with fat yarn tie or pretty ribbon. Be sure & make a hand-written label.

SILENT NIGHT

STILLE NACHT, HEILIGE NACHT

Composed in a few short hours on Christmas eve in 1818, to fill an urgent need for a special Christmas song in a little Bavarian church, this exquisite carol is a Yuletide favorite in practically every language in the Christian world. Its soothing music seems to recreate the very atmosphere of the humble manger birth nearly 2000 years ago.

JOSEPH MÖHR

GERMAN
FRANZ GRÜBER

Calmly with reverence

1. Si - lent night! Ho - ly night! All is calm, all is bright.
2. Si - lent night! Ho - ly night! Shep-herds quake at the sight!
3. Si - lent night! Ho - ly night! Son of God, love's pure light!

Round yon Vir - gin Moth-er and Child! Ho - ly In-fant, so ten-der and mild,
Glo-ries stream from heav-en a - far, Heav'n-ly hosts sing, "Al-le-lu-ia!"
Ra-diant beams from Thy ho - ly face With the dawn of re-deem - ing grace,

Sleep in heav-en-ly peace! Sleep in heav-en-ly peace!
Christ, the Sav-ior, is born! Christ, the Sav-ior, is born!
Je - sus, Lord, at Thy birth! Je - sus, Lord, at Thy birth!

INDEX

Extra:

CAKES:

PICKLES,

PIES:

$\mathcal{S}$

$\mathcal{S}$ALADS:

$\mathcal{S}$IDES:

$\mathcal{S}$OUPS:

About the Author

Dianne Evans wrote her first cookbook in 1964, in Jesup, GA, where she had her own 30 minute daily women's radio show and her listeners sent in recipes that she shared on the air.

Since then, she has authored 6 more cookbooks. She has owned a bakery/catering business and ran several Plantation/Hunting Preserve Main Houses in south Georgia and north Florida. Horseshoe Plantation in Tallahassee, FL and Gillionville Plantation in Albany, GA were two places she cooked for the rich and, often famous, guests of their owners.

One of these owners was John Dorrance, Jr. who later moved the Evans' to Pennsylvania, to perform the resident chef duties at his Gladwyne mansion. Mr. Dorrance's father, who was chemist Dr. John Dorrance, Sr., invented the process for making condensed soup in 1914 after he bought a little soup factory in Camden, N.J. from his uncle. This little soup factory was called the "Joseph Campbell Preserve Company " and later renamed the "Campbell Soup Company".

By special invitation, she and her husband, Emery, were once flown to New York City to serve a southern fried chicken dinner to the Laurence Rockefeller family in the Park Avenue home of Mrs. Caroline Lynch. At the airport, Dianne checked a box of fresh turnip greens along with her luggage and carried her 2 homemade pecan pies in a hatbox on the plane with her. While there, Mrs. Lynch had them cater a luncheon for 70 members of the New York Botanical Society at her Long Island home. For this luncheon, Emery opened a bushel of fresh oysters and made Oysters Rockefeller for the delighted members.

Dianne is the mother of six, grandmother of seven, great-grandmother of three and wife of 50+ years.

Granny Says:
Put your favorite
recipes here:

_____

_____

_____

_____

_____

_____

_____

_____

_____

_____

_____

_____

_____

_____

_____

NOTES